AN ILLUSTRATED GUIDE
to the
MOUNTAIN STREAM INSECTS
of
COLORADO

An Illustrated Guide
to the
MOUNTAIN
STREAM
INSECTS
of COLORADO

Second Edition

J. V. Ward
B. C. Kondratieff
and
R. E. Zuellig

University Press of Colorado

© 2002 by the University Press of Colorado

Published by the University Press of Colorado
5589 Arapahoe Avenue, Suite 206C
Boulder, Colorado 80303

The University Press of Colorado is a cooperative publishing enterprise supported, in part, by Adams State College, Colorado State University, Fort Lewis College, Mesa State College, Metropolitan State College of Denver, University of Colorado, University of Northern Colorado, University of Southern Colorado, and Western State College of Colorado.

The paper used in this publication meets the minimum requirements of the American National Standard for Information Sciences—Permanence of Paper for Printed Library Materials. ANSI Z39.48-1992

Library of Congress Cataloging-in-Publication Data

Ward, James V.
  An illustrated guide to the mountain stream insects of Colorado / James V. Ward, Boris C. Kondratieff, Robert E. Zuellig.— 2nd ed.
    p. cm.
Includes bibliographical references (p.).
  ISBN 0-87081-653-5 (pbk. : alk. paper)
  1. Aquatic insects—Colorado. 2. Aquatic insects—Colorado—Classification. 3. Mountain animals—Colorado. I. Kondratieff, B. C. (Boris C.) II. Zuellig, Robert E. III. Title.
  QL475.C6 W37 2002
  595.716'09788—dc21

                                                                    2001006549

Design by Daniel Pratt

CONTENTS

PREFACE

This guide was written to aid those studying the aquatic insect fauna of Colorado mountain streams. Guides that encompass large geographical areas such as North America must of necessity deal with a highly diverse fauna. By restricting coverage to the mountain streams of Colorado it has been possible to simplify considerably the identification of the aquatic insects that commonly reside in such habitats.

For the first edition, we are grateful to the following: Drs. R. W. Pennak, W. D. Fronk, and R. E. Stevens for reviewing an early draft; Dr. H. E. Evans for reviewing the penultimate draft; D. Hosket-Lundgren for a detailed examination of the literature; E. Bergey, S. Canton, L. Cline, J. Harvey, R. Martinson, D. E. Ruiter, D. Winters, H. Zimmermann, and R. S. Durfee for providing records or identifying specimens; and J. Bodenham, A. Dixon, L. Dunker, R. Hite, P. Jones, M. Kippenhan, T. Sechrist, and J. Stansen for the illustrations. Financial support was provided by a grant from the USDA Forest Service, Rocky Mountain Forest and Range Experiment Station. We thank Mrs. Nadine Kuehl for typing the manuscript.

New material in the second edition includes up-to-date classification and taxonomy of the mountain stream insects of Colorado, and associated literature. Also, additional terms were added to the glossary, and a brief overview of multivariate and multimetric approaches to evaluating water quality are included. Sixteen new figures were added to help illustrate diagnostic characters indicated in the keys.

For the second edition we are grateful to D. E. Ruiter for reviewing the Trichoptera section and providing records and taxonomic expertise and R. S. Durfee for reviewing the Ephemeroptera section and making available his vast knowledge of aquatic insects. Also, we are thankful to D. E. Rees for providing additional species records.

B. C. KONDRATIEFF
J. V. WARD
R. E. ZUELLIG

AN ILLUSTRATED GUIDE
to the
MOUNTAIN STREAM INSECTS
of
COLORADO

INTRODUCTION

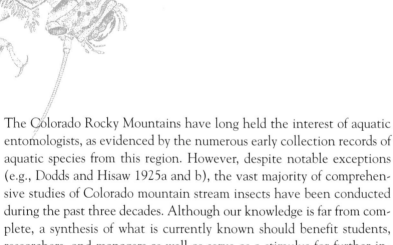

The Colorado Rocky Mountains have long held the interest of aquatic entomologists, as evidenced by the numerous early collection records of aquatic species from this region. However, despite notable exceptions (e.g., Dodds and Hisaw 1925a and b), the vast majority of comprehensive studies of Colorado mountain stream insects have been conducted during the past three decades. Although our knowledge is far from complete, a synthesis of what is currently known should benefit students, researchers, and managers as well as serve as a stimulus for further investigations.

There is no lack of opportunity for investigators to contribute to our knowledge of mountain stream insects of Colorado. The taxonomy of many groups remains to be fully elucidated. Species identification keys for immatures are either unavailable or inadequate for some groups of aquatic insects in this region. Knowledge of distribution patterns within Colorado is also incomplete; only very limited data are available for several major drainage basins. That the distribution of many species is much broader than records indicate becomes readily apparent when collecting in little-studied areas of Colorado. There is also a great need for carefully conducted ecological studies, including analyses of food habits, life history phenomena, and predator-prey interactions, as well as genetic (metapopulation) investigations.

The scope of this volume is limited to the underwater stages of aquatic insects, exclusive of pupae, that reside in Colorado mountain streams. Identification keys are provided for orders, families, and many common genera. Aspects of stream ecology and the major ecological variables influencing aquatic insects precede the identification keys. The impact of humans on mountain stream ecosystems is discussed and the value of aquatic insects as water-quality indicators is considered. Known distributions of species of the three orders for which the most comprehensive data are available (mayflies, stoneflies, and caddisflies) are presented in Appendices A, B, and C. It is intended that this guide not only serve as a source of information for those interested in aquatic insects and mountain streams, but that it also provide a foundation upon which future studies can be built.

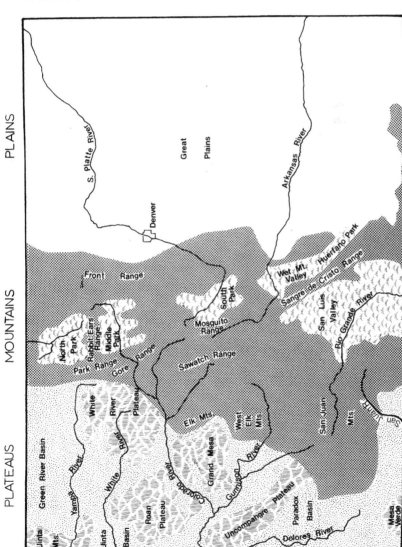

Fig. 1. Map of Colorado showing the three major physiographic regions (greatly modified from Chronic and Chronic 1972).

The
NATURAL SETTING

Colorado may be divided into three general physiographic regions: the Great Plains on the east, the Colorado Plateau on the west, and the Rocky Mountains in between (Fig. 1). Numerous mountain peaks exceed 14,000 ft. (4,267 m) in elevation. Four major rivers have their sources in the Colorado Cordillera. The Colorado River flows into the Pacific Ocean (Gulf of California); the Rio Grande, South Platte, and Arkansas Rivers drain to the Gulf of Mexico.

The topographic diversity and associated gradients in altitude result in five major life zones. These life zones are best exemplified along the easternmost range of mountains in Colorado.

In central Colorado, timberline occurs at about 11,500 ft. (3,505 m), above which lies the Alpine Zone. Protected cirques may contain small glaciers, remnants of the neoglaciation about three thousand years ago. Pristine lakes and clear brooks are set amidst fell-fields and meadows rich in alpine wildflowers.

The Subalpine Zone is dominated by the spruce-fir forest (*Picea engelmannii–Abies lasiocarpa*), which occurs from 10,000 ft. (3,048 m) to timberline.

In the Montane Zone, from 8,000 to 10,000 ft. (2,438–3,048 m), Douglas fir (*Pseudotsuga menziesii*) predominates on north slopes and ponderosa pine (*Pinus ponderosa*) occurs in more xeric locations. Large stands of aspen (*Populus tremuloides*) and lodgepole pine (*Pinus contorta*) also characterize this zone.

The Foothills Zone from 6,000 to 8,000 ft. (1,829–2,438 m) is typified by steep slopes and deep canyons. The Pleistocene glaciers that softened the topography of the Montane Zone did not reach the foothills. Open forests of ponderosa pine occupy mesic sites and shrubs dominate dry slopes. Douglas fir occupies north-facing slopes and Colorado blue spruce occurs in valleys.

The Plains Zone occupies elevations below 6,000 ft. (1,829 m), where grasses are the dominant vegetation of the Great Plains. Trees such as cottonwoods, willows, and boxelder occur only along stream courses.

There are eleven major drainage basins in Colorado, ten of which originate in mountainous regions (Fig. 2). The Yampa, White, Dolores, and San Juan Rivers are subbasins of the Colorado River. The San Luis Valley is a closed basin.

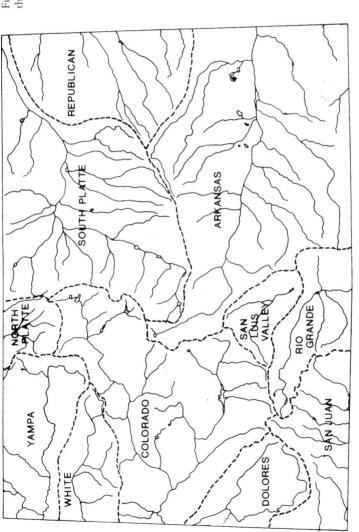

Fig. 2. Map of Colorado showing the eleven major drainage basins.

COLORADO

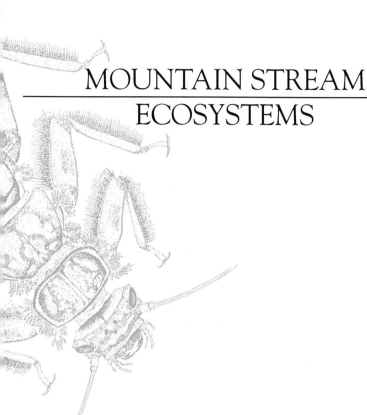

MOUNTAIN STREAM ECOSYSTEMS

A variety of lotic (running water) habitats occur in the mountainous regions of Colorado. Unless otherwise specified, the term "mountain stream" is used broadly to include any lotic system in the western half of Colorado, irrespective of size or elevation. More specific designations (e.g., brook or river) are described later in this section. However, there is an emphasis on the insect fauna characterizing relatively high-gradient rocky-bottomed stream reaches. The remainder of this section briefly summarizes some of the attributes of mountain stream ecosystems. For more detailed accounts see Leopold, Wolman, and Miller (1964), Hynes (1970a), Whitton (1975), Davies and Walker (1986), Ward (1992a and b), Williams and Feltmate (1992), Allan (1995), Leopold (1997), Waters (2000), and Wohl (2000).

SOME BASIC PRINCIPLES

STREAM ORDER ANALYSIS

Stream order (Strahler 1957) is a method of roughly classifying running-water segments by size (Fig. 3). First-order streams are the head-

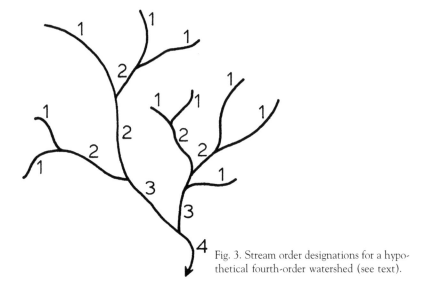

Fig. 3. Stream order designations for a hypothetical fourth-order watershed (see text).

water sources without tributaries. The confluence of two streams of the same order produces the next highest order. Therefore, the joining of two first-order streams produces a second-order segment, two second-order streams produce a third-order stream, and so on. The Mississippi River at its mouth is a twelfth-order stream. The largest rivers in Colorado are eighth- or ninth-order. Although small in size, the lower-order streams are numerous. First- and second-order streams drain about 70 percent of the United States.

LONGITUDINAL PROFILES

The longitudinal profile graphically describes a stream's gradient (slope) as a function of distance from the source. Typically, the longitudinal profile is roughly concave (hyperbolic), with the highest gradient (steepest slope) in the headwaters and the lowest gradient in downstream reaches (Fig. 4).

Although the hydrodynamic phenomena responsible for the concave profile need not concern us here (see Leopold, Wolman, and Miller 1964), the downstream changes in ecological conditions are of interest. For example, the substrate of high-gradient headwater segments is characterized by coarse materials (boulders and rubble), whereas low-gradient downstream reaches may be primarily sand and gravel.

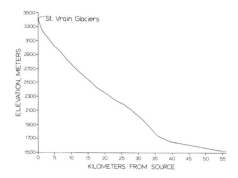

Fig. 4. Longitudinal profile of St. Vrain Creek, Colorado, from alpine tundra (Middle St. Vrain Creek) to the plains.

CHANNEL PATTERNS

There are three major types of channel patterns (Fig. 5). High-gradient mountain streams often flow in relatively straight channels. Even in straight reaches, however, the deepest portion of the stream (the thalweg) tends to move back and forth across the width of the stream. In meandering streams, the entire channel forms S-shaped segments that are continually moving downstream as materials eroded from the concave side are deposited on convex bends. Meander formation requires an erodible substrate and a low gradient. Streams that carry large debris loads tend to form a braided pattern in sections of highly erodible substrate. Such streams are wide and shallow with shifting substrate and numerous islands of various sizes.

RIFFLES AND POOLS

The formation of riffles and pools results from hydrodynamic adjustments of heterogeneous substrate materials to the potential energy of flowing water (Yang 1971). Riffles are shallower and have higher gradients, coarser substrate, and higher current velocities than pools. In natural streams, riffles and pools alternate, with adjacent riffles generally spaced five to seven stream widths apart. Riffles and pools provide quite different habitat conditions for aquatic insects and other organisms.

MAJOR LOTIC HABITAT TYPES

A variety of stream classification and zonation schemes have been proposed (reviewed by Hynes 1970a and Hawkes 1975). The zonation system of Illies and Botosaneanu (1963) and the "River Continuum Concept" of Vannote et al. (1980) are among those most commonly referred to in the literature.

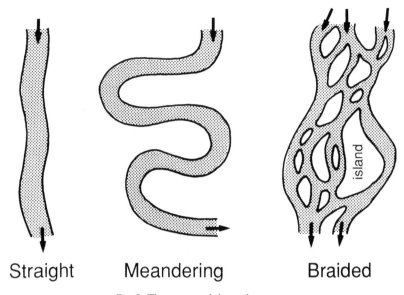

| Straight | Meandering | Braided |

Fig. 5. Three types of channel patterns.

The three major zones in the Illies and Botosaneanu system (Table 1) are based on changes in the benthic invertebrate faunal composition over the longitudinal profile. Crenal includes spring sources and spring brooks (Fig. 6), those generally small lotic habitats dominated by groundwater and often characterized by relatively constant environmental conditions. In Colorado, the upper reaches of river systems, especially those originating at high elevations (Fig. 7), are often fed by surface runoff and snowmelt (rather than groundwater) and may not exhibit many of the characteristics of crenal habitats. Whereas aquatic insects normally make up over 95 percent of the total benthic fauna of high-elevation headwater streams (Short and Ward 1980a; Ward 1986), crenal habitats typically contain few species of insects and an enhanced noninsect invertebrate fauna (Ward and Dufford 1979; Ward, Zimmerman, and Cline 1986).

Rhithral includes the portion of the longitudinal profile from midsize streams to small rivers (Fig. 8). Before the term "crenal" was added to incorporate spring-fed headwaters, rhithral was defined as extending downstream from the source to the location where summer temperatures reach, but do not exceed, 20°C. Other rhithral characteristics include high oxygen concentrations, high current velocities, and coarse

Table 1—Some roughly equivalent terms used to broadly classify lotic habitats and citations of selected studies dealing primarily or exclusively with insects of Colorado mountain stream habitats.

Vernacular Terms	Stream Order	Illies and Botosaneanu (1963)	Vannote et al. (1980)	Selected Colorado Studies
Upper Reaches (brook)	1–3	Crenal	Headwaters	Dodds and Hisaw (1925a, b) Knight and Gaufin (1966) Elgmork and Saether (1970) Mecom (1972a) Allan (1975) Ward and Dufford (1979) Short and Ward (1980a) Ward (1981, 1982, 1986) Ward, Zimmerman, and Cline (1986) Gray et al. (1983)
Middle Reaches (stream)	4–6	Rhithral	Medium-sized Streams	Dodds and Hisaw (1925a, b) Knight and Gaufin (1966) Mecom (1972a) Ward (1981, 1982, 1986) Ward and Berner (1980) Ward, Zimmerman, and Cline (1986) Gray et al. (1983)
Lower Reaches (river)	7–12	Potamal	Large Rivers	Peters and Edmunds (1961) Gaufin and Jensen (1961) Argyle and Edmunds (1962) Knight and Gaufin (1966) Ames (1977) Ward, Zimmerman, and Cline (1986)

substrate. A large portion of the fauna is composed of cold stenotherms, which do not occur in lower reaches because of their intolerance of warm water. The rhithral insect fauna is typified by morphological, behavioral, and physiological adaptations relating to the cold water and rapid current (Hynes 1970a; Ward 1992a).

In potamal segments (Fig. 9), summer water temperatures exceed 20°C, dissolved oxygen may reach low levels during certain periods, the current is slower and less turbulent than in rhithral reaches, and finer

Fig. 6. A spring brook near Fairplay, Colorado. Several beaver ponds are seen in the middle of the photograph. South Park can be seen in the distance (photo by J. V. Ward).

substrate materials predominate. Many of the benthic species occurring in potamal reaches exhibit no special adaptations for running waters and may also inhabit suitable standing-water bodies. Most of the major rivers in Colorado have potamal characteristics in their lower reaches.

The River Continuum Concept (Vannote et al. 1980) hypothesizes that aquatic invertebrates are predictably structured along resource gradients over the longitudinal stream profile. This concept emphasizes downstream shifts in the relative importance of functional feeding groups as the composition of food resources changes along the river continuum. Shredders, which feed on coarse particulate organic matter (CPOM; >1 mm), are hypothesized as being most abundant in headwaters and declining downstream as CPOM (primarily terrestrial leaf litter) concomitantly declines in importance relative to other food resources. Collectors, which utilize fine particulate organic matter (FPOM; <1 mm) in transport (filter feeders) or as sedimentary detritus (gatherers), although also abundant in headwaters, constitute 80–90 percent of the total benthic macroinvertebrates in lower reaches where FPOM dominates the food resources. Scrapers, which feed primarily by grazing on attached algae, are most abundant in middle reaches where in situ

Fig. 7. The headwaters of Middle St. Vrain Creek, Colorado (photo by J. V. Ward).

Fig. 8. The middle reaches of the Frying Pan River upstream from Ruedi Reservoir, Colorado (photo by J. V. Ward).

photosynthesis is highest because of the combination of open canopy and relatively shallow water of high clarity. The relative abundance of invertebrate predators is similar in all reaches, according to the River Continuum Concept.

Whether or not the River Continuum Concept, based primarily on eastern deciduous forest streams, is applicable to Colorado mountain streams remains to be fully elucidated. The more xeric conditions, sparse terrestrial vegetation (low inputs of CPOM), less predictable physical environment, and poor detritus-retention characteristics of high-gradient Colorado streams will undoubtedly modify resource gradients and biotic responses (Fig. 10).

SPECIAL LOTIC HABITATS

In addition to the nonthermal springs (crenal) already mentioned, other special running-water habitats occur in Colorado. The special conditions and fauna of regulated streams—lotic segments below dams—are considered in the section that deals with the impacts of humans on running waters. In this section, discussion will be limited to temporary streams and thermal springs.

Fig. 9. The lower reaches of the Gunnison River, Colorado (photo by J. V. Ward).

Temporary or intermittent streams exhibit surface flow during only a portion of each year (Williams 1987). Aquatic species utilize five strategies to survive the dry phase (Hynes 1970a). Some species survive the dry phase in isolated pools. However, the high temperatures and stagnant conditions in the pools and the vulnerability to predation limit this strategy to only a few species of aquatic insects. Some aquatic insects and other invertebrates burrow into the substrate during the dry phase. Survival does not necessarily require migration to depths where there is liquid water because the interstitial spaces between substrate particles may be saturated with water vapor well above the water table. Several species of aquatic insects have dormant stages (resistant eggs, diapausing larvae) that are resistant to desiccation. Other species complete the aquatic stages of their life cycles and emerge as aerial adults prior to drying of the stream. A few species are highly adapted for temporary waters and employ special tactics: the caddisfly that seals itself in its case to avoid desiccation is one example. Knight and Gaufin (1967) list the species of stoneflies collected from temporary streams in the Gunnison River drainage, but virtually no other research has been conducted on the intermittent streams of Colorado.

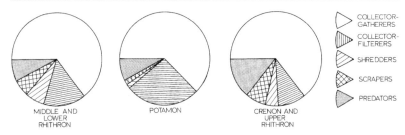

Fig. 10. Changes in the relative contribution of invertebrate functional feeding groups from the upper to the lower reaches of the Colorado River system (modified from Ward, Zimmerman, and Cline 1986).

There are more than a hundred geothermal springs in Colorado (Pearl 1972). Temperatures up to 84°C have been recorded. Most of these springs are small: The largest thermal springs discharge less than 200 liters of water per second. Some of the hot springs have been developed for commercial purposes.

At temperatures of 35–39°C, the fauna consist of a few species each from a few groups that generally occur in hot springs worldwide (Winterbourn 1968). This warm-water fauna comprises primarily eurythermal forms living close to their upper temperature limits. Insect inhabitants include members of several families of true flies (Diptera), damselflies (Odonata), water boatmen and back swimmers (Hemiptera), and dytiscid beetles (Coleoptera). In hot springs (>39°C) the insect fauna is generally restricted to one family of true flies (Ephydridae) and one beetle family (Hydrophilidae). Typical inhabitants of Colorado mountain streams (e.g., stoneflies and mayflies) are not found in thermal springs. Although considerable research has been conducted in the thermal streams in Yellowstone National Park (e.g., Brues 1927; Armitage 1985) and the geyser area of California (e.g., Lamberti and Resh 1983), virtually no data are available on aquatic insects of the thermal waters in Colorado.

CONTROLLING
FACTORS

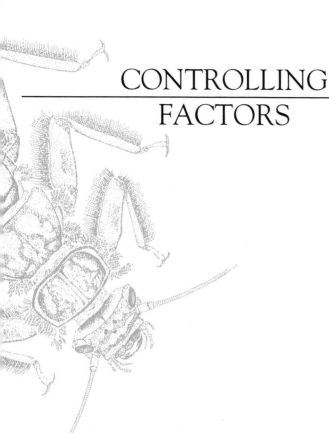

A myriad of environmental factors and their interactions determine the composition and abundance of stream insects. However, in natural streams relatively few major controlling factors account for the environmental variance of primary importance in structuring lotic communities. The remainder of this section addresses these major controlling factors. For additional reading on this topic see Macan (1961, 1974), Hynes (1970a and b), Resh and Rosenberg (1984), Ward (1992a), and Allan (1995).

TEMPERATURE

Spatial and temporal patterns of temperature are extremely important in structuring aquatic insect communities (Ward and Stanford 1982). In addition to latitude and altitude, a variety of hydrological, topographical, and meterological factors are responsible for thermal patterns in streams (Collings 1969; Smith 1972; Smith and Lavis 1975). In natural streams not greatly influenced by groundwater, there is a close relationship between air temperatures and water temperatures except during periods of ice cover, snowmelt, or spates. The aspect of the drainage basin, streamside vegetation, and channel form influence the relative importance of direct solar radiation on stream temperatures (Ward 1985).

Natural streams of mid-latitudes have temperatures that generally vary from around 0° to 25°C or less over an annual cycle. Daily fluctuation of 6°C or more may occur during summer. However, springs often exhibit considerable thermal constancy, with annual ranges of only a few degrees and daily fluctuation of less than 1°C (Ward and Dufford 1979).

Other factors being equal, annual and daily ranges of temperature generally increase from high to low elevations. For example, an annual range of 0–6°C in the headwaters (above timberline) of a Colorado mountain stream contrasted with 0–16°C recorded at a lower foothills location (Ward 1986).

The thermal regime of a lotic system influences distribution patterns, life cycle phenomena, trophic relationships, and behavioral responses of aquatic insects (Ward and Stanford 1982). There are, in addition, many other interactions between temperature and stream fauna, including indirect effects such as the relationship between water temperature and oxygen solubility. Several authors have suggested that altitudinal zonation patterns of stream insects (Fig. 11) result primarily from changes in the temperature regime as a function of elevation (Dodds and Hisaw 1925b; Kamler 1965; Knight and Gaufin 1966; Decamps 1967; Ward and Berner 1980; Ward 1981, 1982, 1984a). Many mountain stream insects are cold stenotherms; some species are able to grow at or near 0°C.

DISCHARGE AND CURRENT

Many lotic insects, especially those of mountain streams, are highly adapted to conditions in running waters, and a large number are restricted to lotic environments because of inherent current requirements associated with their respiratory physiology or feeding mechanisms (Hynes 1970a). Some stream insects cannot survive in still water even if the water is thermally suitable and saturated with oxygen.

Discharge (flow) is a measurement of the volume of water (m³/sec) moving past a given point, whereas current (velocity) is a measurement of the speed (cm/sec) of the flowing water. A current meter directly measures the instantaneous velocity of moving water. Instantaneous

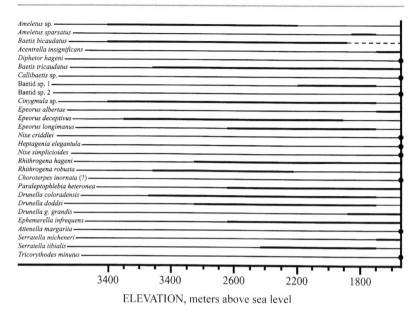

Ameletus sp.
Ameletus sparsatus
Baetis bicaudatus
Acentrella insignificans
Diphetor hageni
Baetis tricaudatus
Callibaetis sp.
Baetid sp. 1
Baetid sp. 2
Cinygmula sp.
Epeorus albertae
Epeorus deceptivus
Epeorus longimanus
Nixe criddlei
Heptagenia elegantula
Nixe simplicioides
Rhithrogena hageni
Rhithrogena robusta
Choroterpes inornata (?)
Paraleptophlebia heteronea
Drunella coloradensis
Drunella doddsi
Drunella g. grandis
Ephemerella infrequens
Attenella margarita
Serratella micheneri
Serratella tibialis
Tricorythodes minutus

3400   3400   2600   2200   1800

ELEVATION, meters above sea level

Fig. 11. The altitudinal zonation of mayflies (Ephemeroptera) in St. Vrain Creek, Colorado (modified from Ward and Berner 1980).

discharge may be estimated by taking a series of current readings across a stream of known depth and width (see John 1978).

Spring-fed streams are characterized by flow constancy, whereas streams fed primarily by runoff typically exhibit extreme flow variation. Most unregulated Colorado mountain streams exhibit snowmelt runoff patterns (Poff and Ward 1989), with relatively predictable annual hydrographs. Peak discharge occurs during the spring snowmelt and minimum flow in late autumn and winter. Mountain streams tend to be liable to spates and may exhibit orders-of-magnitude change in discharge as a result of major storm events.

Current velocity decreases from the water surface to the streambed and is generally lower near the banks than in the center of the stream. Stream insects may partition the habitat according to current preference, with species well adapted to current residing primarily in the center of the stream and species poorly adapted to current being restricted to the edges (Needham and Usinger 1956). The microcurrent regime near the streambed is of interest because it is the habitat of most lotic insects. Near-bed hydraulic conditions in high-gradient mountain

Table 2—A simplified classification of mineral substrate particle sizes.

Substrate Category	Range of Particle Size (mm)
Boulder	>256
Cobble	64–256
Pebble	16–64
Gravel	2–16
Sand	0.0625–2
Silt	0.0039–0.0625
Clay	<0.0039

streams are turbulent with extremely complex patterns (Davis and Barmuta 1989).

SUBSTRATE AND SUSPENDED MATTER

The substrate composition, nature, and amount of materials in transport are largely a function of the area geology and the flow regime of natural streams. Erosional streams (or erosional areas of streams) have sufficient current to remove fine substrate particles (see Table 2 for substrate size categories). Consequently, erosional areas such as riffles have a predominance of coarse substrate materials, whereas the substrate of depositional areas such as pools is composed largely of fine particles such as sand and silt. Because stream insects are benthic organisms (i.e., closely associated with a substrate), the structure of communities in depositional and erosional areas may differ considerably. Even within a single riffle the composition and standing crops of benthic organisms vary according to specific substrate type (Table 3).

It should be emphasized that the substrate of a stream is nearly always a mixture of various sizes of mineral particles and organic detritus (Minshall 1984). The detrital component serves as a food resource for many stream insects, as is described in the next section. Stream insects vary greatly in their substrate preferences. For example, some species of burrowing mayflies are restricted to substrate with a narrow range of particle sizes, whereas other species of mayflies occur on a wide range of substrate types.

The concentration of suspended matter in Colorado mountain streams is directly related to discharge. Streams that are extremely clear at low flow may carry large quantities of suspended matter during spring runoff or following major storm events. The insects of mountain streams

Table 3—The relative contributions of the insect orders to total numbers of insects on four substrate types in North St. Vrain Creek, Colorado.

Insect Order	Sand	Percentage Composition Gravel	Cobble	Bedrock
Ephemeroptera	61	71	63	34
Plecoptera	+	10	5	+
Trichoptera	6	8	23	19
Coleoptera	+	4	2	+
Diptera	32	7	7	46
Average insects/m^2	(85)	(244)	(265)	(136)

Source: Modified from Ward 1975. Note: + = less than 1%.

are able to withstand normal variations in discharge and concomitant changes in suspended loads, although severe floods or alterations induced by humans may have devastating effects on the fauna.

CHEMICAL CONDITIONS

Although aquatic insects are affected by chemical conditions, natural variations in water chemistry are rarely as important as temperature, flow, or substrate in structuring stream communities. Only under special circumstances (e.g., saline streams) does water chemistry have an overriding effect on aquatic insects of unpolluted Colorado mountain streams. Chemical conditions play a much greater biological role in standing waters. See Golterman (1975) for a review of the chemistry of stream water. The present account is restricted to very brief considerations of total dissolved solids (TDS), dissolved gases, and nutrients.

TOTAL DISSOLVED SOLIDS

The headwaters of streams originating near the Continental Divide in regions of insoluble bedrock (granite, schist, gneiss) often contain extremely soft water (<10 mg/l TDS) and thus exhibit low biotic productivity. Ionic concentrations increase as the water flows downstream (especially if exposed to sedimentary rock) and begin at much higher levels in streams originating in areas of more soluble rock types. The world's rivers contain an average total salinity of 120 mg/l (Wetzel 1983).

Streams fed primarily by surface runoff generally exhibit an inverse relationship between flow and the TDS concentration. At low flow, more of the water has contact with the substrate over a longer period.

Pennak (1977) reported order-of-magnitude temporal changes in TDS values in some soft-water Rocky Mountain streams. Colorado mountain streams tend to be highly turbulent; thus chemical constituents tend to be well mixed. In contrast, standing-water bodies may exhibit chemical stratification during stagnant periods.

DISSOLVED GASES

Turbulence also accounts for the fact that dissolved gases, such as oxygen and carbon dioxide, are normally in equilibrium with the atmosphere. Low oxygen and high CO_2 levels are characteristic of organically polluted waters but occur only under special circumstances in natural streams. The sources of certain spring-fed streams exhibit low levels of oxygen, as do some small streams that receive large inputs of leaf litter (natural organic pollution) over a short time interval. Many stream insects have evolved in habitats where oxygen levels are always near saturation. Unlike related species in lakes and ponds, these insects have not developed adaptations for tolerating low levels of oxygen, even for short periods.

NUTRIENT SALTS

Nitrates and phosphates are the major nutrients of biological importance that may be limiting in natural waters. Both typically occur in trace amounts and may be taken up rapidly by aquatic plants. The importance of plant nutrients to aquatic insects is through their influence on the food base (primarily producers). Because of turbulence, local depletions in dissolved nutrients tend not to occur in running waters. Running waters are said to be "physiologically richer" than standing waters partly because the current makes nutrients more readily available to organisms (Ruttner 1926). Cultural eutrophication of water bodies results from increases in plant nutrients and from pollution, agricultural runoff, and several other sources.

AQUATIC AND RIPARIAN VEGETATION

Stream flora may be conveniently, if somewhat artificially, grouped into the following three categories: algae, aquatic macrophytes, and riparian (streamside) vegetation. Comprehensive treatments of stream flora include Hynes (1970a), Hutchinson (1975), Westlake (1975), Haslam (1978), Lock et al. (1984), Cummins et al. (1989), Gregory et al. (1991), Malanson (1993), and Naiman and Decamps (1997).

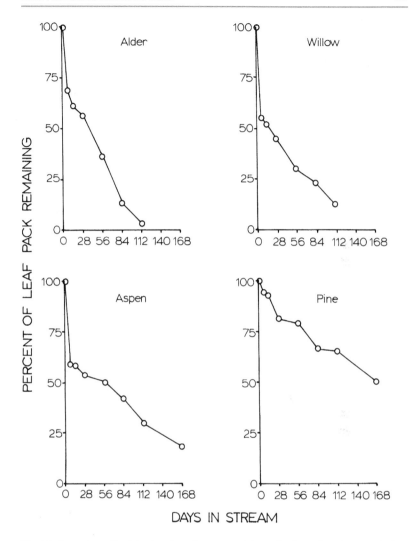

Fig. 12. Processing of leaf detritus from four terrestrial woody plants, based on weight loss of preweighed leaf packs (modified from Short, Canton, and Ward 1980).

Aquatic macrophytes of rocky-bottomed, high-gradient Colorado mountain streams are primarily limited to mosses, lichens, and liverworts. Submerged angiosperms are generally restricted to lower-gradient downstream reaches or to special lotic habitats such as spring brooks or streams below dams. Few aquatic invertebrates utilize submerged angiosperms for food, at least while the plants are alive; this is especially true of stream insects (Hynes 1970a). However, algae that are fed upon by animals colonize the stems and leaves of higher aquatic plants. In addition, higher plants create current refugia, provide case-building materials, and, upon senescence, serve as food for detritivorous insects (Minshall 1978).

The term "periphyton" is commonly used for the assemblage of algae attached to submerged surfaces (rocks, logs, and leaves and stems of higher aquatic plants). Diatoms and green and blue-green algae are major components. Bacteria and other microorganisms are also associated with submerged surfaces, and fine organic detritus is entrapped by the latticework of living cells. Many stream insects are adapted to exploit this rich and concentrated food resource.

In mountain streams the action of spring runoff tends to scour rock surfaces, resulting in a seasonal pattern of algal abundance. However, even under the constant conditions of spring brooks, distinct temporal patterns may be apparent (Ward and Dufford 1979). Unlike aquatic angiosperms, many species of algae are restricted to running waters and some are even confined to rapids (Hynes 1970a).

The riparian zone may be thought of as the ecotone between the stream proper and the terrestrial environment. Riparian vegetation reduces bank erosion, buffers the stream from extreme temperature fluctuations, provides resting and oviposition sites for aerial stages of aquatic insects, and contributes leaf litter and other forms of detritus to the energy budget of the lotic ecosystem.

The riparian vegetation of Colorado mountain streams varies as a function of altitude. In alpine tundra, forbs and grasses often form dense stands on the stream banks and may be accompanied by dwarf willows and birch. Various willow shrubs and Rocky Mountain alder form narrow riparian zones at middle and lower elevations. In the Montane and Foothills Zones, riparian trees (cottonwoods and willows) may also occur on the narrow floodplains. Both riparian and nonriparian species contribute to the detrital pool of the stream, thus providing a sequence of decomposition rates (Fig. 12).

INSECTS *of*
AQUATIC HABITATS

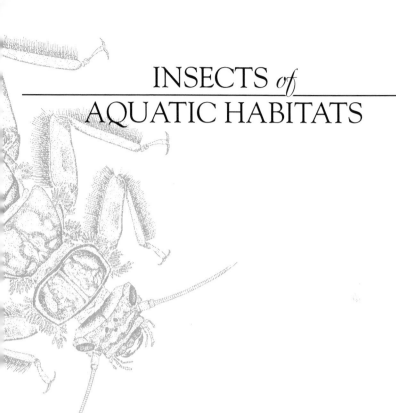

Cool headwater streams apparently served as an ancestral habitat for many major groups of aquatic insects, of which some lineages later adapted to standing waters and warmer lotic reaches downstream (Ross 1956; Hynes 1970a). An appreciation of this evolutionary heritage is necessary for a fuller understanding of the distribution and ecology of mountain stream insects. In this section, a discussion of the salient features of aquatic-insect life histories and food habits is followed by a brief description of the behavioral and morphological adaptations of stream insects.

LIFE HISTORIES

Aquatic insects exhibit two types of metamorphosis (changing form). The primitively wingless springtails (not regarded as true insects by some authorities) are ametabolous, which means that there is no change in body form from the time of hatching to maturity. Aquatic bugs (Hemiptera) are said to be paurometabolous (undergo gradual metamorphosis). The immatures of paurometabolous insects are called nymphs. Except for the absence of wings, the nymphs are very similar in structure to the adults. Nymphs and adults reside in the same habitat and have similar food habits. Stoneflies, dragonflies, and mayflies are hemimetabolous (undergo incomplete metamorphosis). The immatures, termed nymphs, are aquatic, whereas the adults are terrestrial. Some entomologists do not use the term "nymph," but instead refer to the immatures of all insects as larvae (Edmunds, Jensen, and Berner 1976, pp. 45–46). Immatures and adults of hemimetabolous insects live in different habitats and exhibit different feeding habits, thus eliminating direct intraspecific competition between life stages. Morphological studies have indicated that although Odonata and Ephemeroptera show some evolutionary relationships with each other, they are not related to the Plecoptera; therefore, these three orders are not a cohesive phylogenetic group. The paurometabolous and hemimetabolous groups have therefore been abandoned and the two merged under the heading *hemimetabolous*. Mayflies are unique among insects in that they have two winged stages. The subimago (subadult) is produced by the final nymphal molt. The subimago is terrestrial and fully winged but is usually not sexually mature. After a few minutes to several days (depending on the species and weather conditions), the thin exocuticle covering the wings and body of the subimago is shed and the imago emerges. Whereas the subimago (called a "dun" by anglers) has a dull body and translucent wings, the imago is shiny with transparent wings. (These are called "spinners" by anglers.)

The remaining orders of aquatic insects are *holometabolous* (undergo complete metamorphosis). The larvae that hatch from the eggs of holometabolous insects are dramatically different from the adults. Unlike nymphs, larvae lack external wing buds, and legs are reduced or absent. The nonfeeding and sometimes-quiescent pupa is a transitional stage in holometabolous insects. The representatives of most orders of holometabolous insects (e.g., caddisflies, aquatic moths, dipterans, dobson flies) are aquatic as larvae and terrestrial as adults. Most aquatic beetles, however, are aquatic in both larval and adult stages. The mature larvae of most beetles (and some other groups of aquatic insects) crawl out of the water and construct pupal chambers on land. Upon transformation to the adult stage most aquatic beetles return to the water. Adult beetles and bugs may leave the water for dispersal flights.

The eggs of aquatic insects are laid on the water surface, underwater, above the water surface in association with plants, or in damp marginal areas. The aerial adults of some insects crawl underwater to deposit eggs. The adults of some aquatic bugs and beetles attach the eggs to their bodies.

The term "voltinism" refers to the number of generations completed per year. A univoltine life cycle, one generation per year, is the common pattern among stream insects in temperate regions (Hynes 1970a). Semivoltine and perennial species require two or more than two years, respectively, to complete one generation. Species exhibiting univoltinism at low elevations (or latitudes) may be semivoltine or even perennial at high elevations (or latitudes). Bivoltine and multivoltine species complete two and more than two generations, respectively, during each annual cycle. Species exhibiting more than one generation per year are most common in warm climates or in constant thermal environments such as spring brooks. See Landa (1968) and Hynes (1970a) for detailed discussion of life cycle phenomena of aquatic insects.

FOOD AND FEEDING

Stream insects tend to be food generalists that vary the type of material ingested at least partly in response to food availability (Cummins 1973). Therefore, the gut contents of many lotic species generally reflect the proportions of the various food items present in the habitat, which vary from stream to stream as well as spatially and seasonally in the same stream. This adaptability is in stark contrast to terrestrial insects, many species of which are highly specialized feeders. The food habits of stream insects also vary with age; most species feed on fine organic detritus upon hatching from the egg irrespective of the food habits of later stages.

There are, of course, exceptions to the catholic food habits of stream insects and some diet selectivity does indeed occur (Gray and Ward 1979). For example, living aquatic angiosperms tend not to be eaten and their relative abundance in lotic habitats will not be reflected in gut analyses.

Food habits of stream insects tend to be based more on feeding mechanisms (functional feeding groups) than on selection of specific food types (Cummins 1973). Table 4 shows the categories of food resources available in lotic ecosystems and the macroinvertebrate functional feeding groups utilizing each resource. See Merritt and Cummins

Table 4—Categories of organic resources in streams and the major functional feeding groups using the resources.

Category Range	General Size	Major Source	Macroinvertebrate Functional Feeding Group
Periphyton	10–500μm	In-stream Production	Scrapers
Macrophytes	> 1 cm	In-stream production	Herbivore Shredders
Detritus			
CPOM	> 1 mm		
Woody		Terrestrial Plants	Gougers, Detritivore Shredders
Nonwoody		Terrestrial Plants	Detritivore Shredders
FPOM	0.5μm–1 mm	Upstream, CPOM Processing, DOM Flocculation	Collectors
DOM	< 0.5μm	Upstream, Leaching, Metabolites	None
Animals		In-stream growth	Predators

Source: Modified from Cummins (1979).
Note: CPOM = Coarse Particulate Organic Matter; FPOM = Fine Particulate Organic Matter; DOM = Dissolved Organic Matter.

(1996) for a tabular summary of the known feeding mechanism of North American genera of aquatic insects.

Some of the functional feeding groups were briefly referred to in the previous section of this book entitled "Major Lotic Habitat Types" (see also Fig. 10); their definitions are repeated here for the sake of clarity. Scrapers feed on periphyton, which is the assemblage of algae, bacteria, other microorganisms, and entrapped detritus attached to or intimately associated with solid surfaces (e.g., rocks, wood). The mouthparts of scrapers are structurally suited for rasping. Shredders are adapted to feed on relatively large organic particles (Table 4). Herbivore shredders feed on living macrophytes; detritivore shredders feed on coarse particulate organic matter (CPOM), and associated microbes, of primarily terrestrial origin. Gougers are specialized for boring in submerged wood (Anderson et al. 1978). Collectors feed on fine particulate organic matter (FPOM). Filter-feeding collectors construct nets or use hair fringes or other devices to remove the FPOM carried in transport by the flowing water (Wallace and Merritt 1980). Collector-gatherers are deposit feeders adapted to utilize sedimentary organic matter. Predators are adapted for capturing and consuming other animals, which are nor-

Table 5—Some morphological and behavioral adaptations of aquatic insects to life in running waters.

Adaptation	Ecological Implications	Example
MORPHOLOGICAL		
Flattening	Current avoidance (reside in boundary layer or crevices)	heptageniid mayflies
Small Size	Current avoidance (reside in boundary layer or crevices)	elmid beetles
Streamlining	Smooth surfaces and fusiform shape offer least resistance to current	baetid mayflies
Suckers	Can live on tops of rocks in rapid current	blepharicerids (net-winged midge)
Friction Pads	Increased body contact increases frictional resistance	*Drunella doddsi* (mayfly)
Claws and Hooks	Reduced chance of dislodgement (mountain midge)	deuterophlebiids
Silk and Sticky Secretions	Attach to object in rapid current	*Simulium arcticum* (black fly)
BEHAVIORAL		
Ballast	Attach rocks to cases to reduce buoyancy	certain cased caddisflies
Positive Rheotaxis	Tendency to move against current counters downstream displacement	leptophlebiid mayflies
Negative Phototaxis	Current avoidance by cryptic behavior	*Paraperla frontalis* (stonefly)
Current Preferenda	Selection of areas of suitable current	caenid mayflies

Source: Modified from Hynes (1970a).

mally consumed whole or in large pieces. A few predators, however, are adapted for piercing their prey and sucking out the body fluids.

Specific examples of these feeding mechanisms are presented in the next section. Several studies have dealt with food habits of insects in Colorado mountain streams (Richardson and Gaufin 1971; Mecom 1972b; Fuller and Stewart 1977, 1979; Gray and Ward 1979; Short, Canton, and Ward 1980; Short and Ward 1980b, 1981; Allan 1982; Martinson and Ward 1982; Rader and Ward 1987a).

ADAPTATIONS TO RUNNING WATERS

Lotic insects are of necessity highly adapted to living in (or avoiding) current (Table 5). Although morphological and behavioral adaptations function in concert, it is convenient to discuss them separately. The examples refer to figures in the section on identification. Flattening of the body is a common evolutionary adaptation for insects residing in rapid streams. A highly flattened insect can presumably move over the surfaces of rocks in very rapid water and yet not be exposed to the current. The mayfly family Heptageniidae, an important faunal component of Colorado mountain streams, provides the best examples of flattening (see Figs. 43a, 45). Flattening also enables aquatic insects to move into crevices to avoid current (and predators). Numerous species of stream insects are cryptic during the day, moving to the surfaces of stones only under cover of darkness. A few insects in depositional areas also exhibit flattening: it enables them to stay on the surface of soft substrates.

If an insect is small enough, it is able to avoid the current or live in crevices without being flattened. Elmid beetles (see Figs. 88, 89), often the only coleopterans of mountain streams, are much smaller than members of other families of beetles that occur in slow streams or lentic water bodies.

Research on the hydraulic forces to which stream insects are exposed (e.g., Statzner and Holme 1989) necessitates a critical reexamination of these purported morphological adaptations to current. It appears that even highly flattened or very small species may pay considerable energetic costs during incursions to current-exposed microhabitats.

Some lotic insects use streamlining and some species also possess the fusiform body shape exhibited by trout. The fusiform shape, when combined with a reduction of body projections, offers the least resistance to current. Certain baetid mayflies (see Fig. 49) are good examples of stream insects that are able to colonize the upper surfaces of rocks in rapid water because of their streamlined bodies. Other mayflies living in slower currents or lentic waters may also be streamlined (see Fig. 56); however, the streamlining in these cases serves to reduce resistance when swimming.

Another adaptation enabling insects to reside on the tops of rocks in rapid water is the possession of suckers or friction pads. Net-winged midges (Blephariceridae) possess hydraulic suckers on the ventral body surface (see Fig. 90) that allow these highly specialized larvae to maintain their positions and even move upstream on smooth rock surfaces in extremely rapid water. The mayfly *Drunella doddsi* has an elaborate hair pad on the ventral abdominal surface (see Fig. 40b) that increases frictional resistance with the substrate. The gills of the mayfly genus *Rhithrogena* are positioned to form a ventral friction device (see Fig. 43b). The labrum (upper lip) of some mayflies is enlarged, flattened, and fringed with hairs (see Fig. 45). By appressing their heads to the substrate, nymphs prevent water from flowing under their bodies and dislodging them. The mayflies may thus feed on periphyton on the tops of rocks in rapid water.

Numerous stream insects have well-developed claws and hooks that allow them to maintain position in current. The tarsal claws are well developed on the legs of many lotic species, although dipteran larvae lack true legs. Dipterans may, however, have prolegs or pseudopods with terminal hooks (see Figs. 91, 95, 99); larval black flies also have a circlet of hooks on the flattened apex of the abdomen (only partly visible in the lateral view in Fig. 92). Many caddisflies have claws on posterior prolegs that are used to prevent dislodgement from their cases. The caddisfly genus *Rhyacophila*, however, does not possess a larval case and uses the hooked prolegs to cling to the substrate (see Fig. 69).

Some insects use silk and sticky secretions to maintain position in current. Larval black flies attach a mat of interwoven silk to the substrate to which they attach themselves by means of the posterior circlet of hooks. In addition, they spin a "safety line" of silk that is used during accidental or purposeful (predator avoidance) dislodgement. Upon releasing themselves from their normal feeding position, they swing out in the current on the end of the "safety line." They subsequently are able to work their way back to their original position using the silken strand for guidance and support. Black flies pupate in a silken case (see Fig. 92) attached to the substrate in flowing water. Some midges and other insects also spin silken tubes. The larval cases and feeding nets of some caddisflies are permanently attached to the substrate. Some caddis larvae with portable cases temporarily anchor themselves to the substrate. *Brachycentrus americanus* (see Fig. 61) uses silk to temporarily attach its case to the substrate to free its legs for feeding activities. Many species of stream caddisflies use silk to attach their cases to rocks and other objects when molting and during the quiescent pupal stage. The eggs of stream insects often either are attached to the substrate during oviposition or possess adhesive surfaces or special attachment structures.

Ballast involves mechanisms to increase density. Stream-dwelling caddisflies tend to construct heavier cases than lentic species, and a few lotic species attach large stones to their portable cases to increase density (and to reduce the chances of being swept away), especially during the pupal stage.

Many stream insects, if not most, are positively rheotactic; that is, they tend to face into the current. This position not only reduces their chances of being swept away but also means that locomotion tends to be primarily in the upstream direction. In addition, the adults of many stream insects exhibit a propensity to fly in the upstream direction, thus further compensating for the downstream displacement of aquatic stages by the current (Müller 1982).

The negative phototaxis of many lotic insects results in current avoidance through cryptic behavior during the day. During the hours of darkness, aquatic insects may leave the substrate interstices and become more exposed to the current, which in part explains the night peaks in drift (downstream displacement of organisms by current) exhibited by the majority of species.

Many stream insects exhibit current preferenda that roughly correspond to their abilities to maintain position in running waters. Species poorly adapted to resist current tend to reside in weed beds or along the edges of streams, where current velocity is reduced.

IMPACTS *of* HUMANS *on* MOUNTAIN STREAMS

A stream is an integral component of the watershed through which it flows (Hynes 1975). The stream environment reflects the geochemical and meteorological conditions, the prevailing terrestrial vegetation, and other characteristics of the watershed. Any major alterations of watershed characteristics, whether natural or induced by humans, have an influence on the stream environment. Wohl (2001) provides an excellent overview of anthropogenic influences on mountain rivers along the Front Range of Colorado.

Covich et al. (1995, p. 5) defines ecological integrity from a western water manager's perspective as an "ecosystem where interconnected elements of physical habitat, and the processes that create and maintain them, are capable of supporting and sustaining the full range of biota adapted for that region." This section briefly summarizes some of the ways that humans degrade the ecological integrity of mountain streams and the consequent effects on habitat conditions and aquatic insect communities.

AQUATIC INSECTS AND WATER QUALITY

Aquatic insects and other macroinvertebrates have several attributes not possessed by other water quality indicators (Goodnight 1973; Wilhm and Dorris 1968; Hawkes 1979; Rosenberg and Resh 1993). Aquatic insects, unlike physical and chemical parameters (unless continuously monitored), reflect not only present but also past and extreme environmental conditions. They are not as freely mobile as fishes, which can immediately recolonize an area when conditions improve. Aquatic insects do not present the special problems in collection and identification that are so characteristic of microorganisms. They provide some information on water quality, even at a fairly coarse level of taxonomic resolution. In addition, the life cycles of aquatic insects are generally of a duration to provide maximum information on environmental conditions. The implication is not to depend solely on one component (e.g., aquatic insects) in assessing stream conditions, but to be aware of the limitations of the various components sampled.

STREAM REGULATION

When a dam is placed on a previously free-flowing stream (Fig. 13), the inundated portion behind the dam is not the only stream segment that is altered. Environmental conditions in the remaining lotic reaches may be greatly influenced by the impoundment upstream. Specific changes in the downstream environment depend on the interactions of many factors, such as the depth from which water is released at the dam and operational variables (Ward and Stanford 1979; Petts 1984). In some cases distinct adverse effects are apparent, such as when anaerobic waters are released downstream. In other cases the biotic changes are a function of more subtle, sublethal alterations, often resulting from modifications of the natural temperature and flow regimes.

Deep-release dams tend to suppress natural thermal variation in the stream reach below the impoundment. Aquatic organisms with strict thermal requirements may thus be eliminated from regulated streams (Ward 1976a). Flow regime alterations vary primarily according to the purposes of the reservoir. For example, discharge exhibits extreme short-term fluctuation below hydroelectric dams, whereas storage reservoirs tend to dampen short- and long-term extremes (Ward 1976b).

In the absence of adverse conditions such as oxygen deficits, the species diversity of stream macroinvertebrates tends to be moderately

Fig. 13. Buttonrock Dam (64 m high; deep release; capacity 20 x 10⁶ m³) on North St. Vrain Creek, Colorado (photo by J. V. Ward).

reduced below Colorado mountain reservoirs but gradually recovers as the temperature regime and other factors approach normal levels (Fig. 14). Stoneflies are often severely reduced immediately below dams, whereas dipterans (especially chironomids) increase in relative abundance. Some insect orders, while not changing greatly in relative abundance (compared to unregulated streams), exhibit major taxonomic shifts. For example, *Baetis* increases and heptageniid mayflies are reduced or eliminated in regulated streams. Noninsects, such as amphipods, snails, oligochaetes, and turbellarians, tend to increase in relative abundance in regulated stream reaches.

The effects of stream regulation on macroinvertebrate standing crop are variable and largely dependent upon the flow regime. Enhanced flow constancy, if not associated with excessive sedimentation, may result in large increases in the density and biomass of stream benthos. High abundance values may also occur below hydroelectric dams if daily flow fluctuations are not severe and if annual flow constancy is enhanced by regulation. Extremely high standing crops of filter-feeding insects, such as black flies and hydropsychid caddisflies, characterize stream segments below surface-release reservoirs and natural lakes.

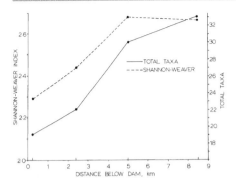

Fig. 14. The depression and downstream recovery of macroinvertebrate diversity in the South Platte River below Cheesman Reservoir, Colorado (modified from Ward 1976a).

ORGANIC POLLUTION

The effect of organic pollution on aquatic insects is well documented, at least in Europe and eastern North America (Hynes 1960; Wiederholm 1984; Giller and Malmqvist 2000). Although many factors and complex interactions are involved, the reduced dissolved-oxygen levels downstream from sewage effluents play a major role in shaping the biotic community. Because mountain stream insects evolved in habitats typified by high levels of oxygen, most are eliminated by any significant reductions in dissolved oxygen. Organisms able to tolerate low-oxygen conditions may, however, build up extremely large populations because of the abundant food resources and the reduced competition and predation. Some species of chironomids (see Fig. 108) are called "bloodworms" because they have hemoglobin in solution in the blood, which enables them to efficiently extract oxygen from low-oxygen waters (Walshe 1950). Other insect larvae found in polluted waters, such as "rat-tailed maggots" (see Fig. 101), do not rely on dissolved oxygen but have elongated respiratory tubes and breathe atmospheric air.

Streams receiving organic pollution may be divided into zones according to the severity of conditions. The lengths of the zones vary depending on the organic input, stream discharge, season, and a myriad of other factors. In the clean-water zone, upstream from the input of sewage, species diversity is high, although faunal density is relatively low. In the zone of degradation, immediately below a major sewage effluent, insects and other invertebrates are normally absent, the biota being composed primarily of bacteria. The zone of active decomposition is characterized by somewhat higher oxygen levels and a high biomass comprising few species. Sewage "fungus," an assemblage of bacteria, fungi, and protozoans, forms dense masses. *Chironomus* (blood-worms), *Eristalis* (rat-tailed maggots), and tubuficid worms often attain high densities in this zone. With additional distance the stream enters the zone of recovery, sometimes referred to as the *Cladophora/Asellus* zone because of the predominant plant and animal components. Although still low, macroinvertebrate species diversity is higher than in the previous zone. The aquatic insect fauna is limited to a few species that are able to tolerate low nighttime oxygen levels. Because of the dense plant growth (resulting from high levels of plant nutrients), dissolved oxygen may reach supersaturation during the day. With further distance downstream, recovery is complete and a normal clean-water fauna and flora again predominate.

MINING

With regard to effects on mountain streams, mining in Colorado must be separated into at least two major categories. Acid mine drainage is generally associated with metal mines, whereas streams that drain energy mines tend not to be acidic. The reasons for these differences, and the contrasting effects on lotic insects, are considered in this section.

Heavy-metal pollution associated with acid mine drainage is considered one of the most significant environmental problems in Colorado Rocky Mountain streams (Colorado Department of Health 1992; Clements et al. 2000). It is estimated that heavy-metal pollution from approximately ten thousand abandoned mining sites affects over 2,600 kilometers of streams in Colorado (Colorado Department of Health 1992). Clements et al. (2000) has shown that heavy metals from these abandoned mines are major factors structuring benthic communities. Acid mine drainage damages the stream environment in three major ways. First, low pH per se stresses aquatic insects and other organisms; second, ferric hydroxide precipitate blankets the substrate; and third, heavy-metal solubility and toxicity are normally highest under acidic conditions.

Severe acid mine drainage eliminates aquatic insects for varying distances below the point at which the effluent enters the stream. Downstream biotic recovery depends on several factors but is closely associated with the extent to which pH approaches normal levels (Gray and Ward 1983). Typical changes to the benthic community include reduced abundance, reduced species richness, and community composition shifts from metal-sensitive to metal-tolerant organisms (Clements and Kiffney 1994). Although few field studies have been conducted, published data (Peckarsky and Cook 1981; McKnight and Feder 1984) suggest that acid mine drainage has similar effects on aquatic insects of Colorado mountain streams as reported for streams in the midwestern and eastern states.

In contrast to metal mine drainage, drainage from coal mines alters water quality and aquatic insects of Colorado mountain streams much less severely (Wentz 1974; Ward, Canton, and Gray 1978). Acid mine drainage and ferric hydroxide precipitation are rarely associated with streams adjacent to coal mines in Colorado, partly because of the low sulfate content of western coal. Even where sulfate levels are higher, the alkaline, highly buffered waters reduce acid formation and the solubility of heavy metals. Water depletion, sedimentation, and increased salinity appear to be the major potential problems associated with western coal mining. With proper environmental safeguards, the effects of coal mining on the aquatic insects of Colorado mountain streams are relatively minor compared to the alterations engendered by metal mine drainage (Ward, Canton, and Gray 1978; Canton and Ward 1981b).

OTHER WATERSHED DISTURBANCES

Ward (1984b) has reviewed how various alterations of the watershed influence aquatic insects and how ecologically sound management strategies can minimize adverse effects. Alterations not already addressed in this section are briefly discussed here. However, few data are available that specifically relate such alterations to the insect fauna of Colorado mountain streams.

Several land-use practices often result in the removal of vegetation along streams. Terrestrial vegetation, through inputs of leaf detritus, provides an important energy source, especially for small streams. Riparian plants also provide oviposition and resting sites for aerial stages of aquatic insects. Watersheds affected by disturbances such as logging often exhibit dramatic increases in sediment and nutrient losses to adjacent waters. Removal of riparian vegetation may also dramatically increase annual and diet ranges of stream temperature with attendant effects on aquatic insects. Recovery of aquatic-insect communities from alterations resulting from watershed disturbances appears to be directly related to the recovery rates of terrestrial vegetation. However, relatively narrow buffer strips (i.e., corridors where streamside vegetation is protected from logging, grazing, or other disruption) quite effectively protect the stream ecosystem from changes in the thermal regime, erosion, and the like.

A long-term study of a high mountain stream in Colorado demonstrated the recovery potential of lotic ecosystems (Cline, Short, and Ward 1982). Although suspended solids exhibited ten- to hundredfold increases over reference levels at stream sites influenced by highway construction activities, levels rapidly returned to normal following cessation of construction. Stream insects were measurably affected by localized impacts at some locations, but not others, and recovered fairly rapidly at affected sites. The relatively high inertia (resistance to change) and resilience (recovery following alteration) were attributed to several factors. Construction activities directly affecting the stream were localized (e.g., bridge construction) and relatively short-term events. Undisturbed areas occurred above impacted sites and in tributaries. Construction did not appreciably alter the thermal or flow regimes or the water chemistry. The highest concentrations of suspended solids occurred during spring runoff, which, combined with the steep stream gradient, prevented sedimentation in the study reach.

Sediment also deposits behind the dams of reservoirs, which needs to be flushed periodically so that the reservoir maintains storage capacity. A recent example of this in Colorado occurred in September 1996 when approximately 7,000 cubic meters of clay to gravel-sized sediment was released from Halligan Reservoir on the North Fork of the Cache la Poudre River. The sediment release filled pools as far as 10 kilometers downstream of the reservoir (Wohl and Cenderell 2000). Initially, benthic macroinvertebrates were eliminated directly below the dam and were greatly reduced to distances up to 3.2 kilometers downstream when compared with pre-event data. Macroinvertebrate densities recovered quickly as flows increased and sediment began to move, but community function had not recovered to pre-event conditions two years after the release (Zuellig, Kondratieff, and Rhodes, 2002). Waters (1995) provides an excellent review of the effect of sediment on aquatic communities.

The unidirectional flow of running waters, combined with the multiple colonization pathways of aquatic insects, greatly enhances the recovery potential of lotic ecosystems, assuming that the functional

integrity of the stream is maintained. Streams must be especially protected from alterations such as channelization and from residual toxi-
cants, such as certain pesticides and heavy metals, that may alter the
ecosystem structure and function for many years.

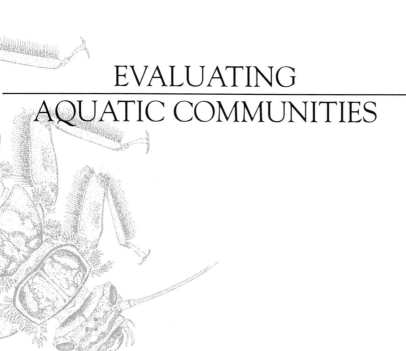

EVALUATING
AQUATIC COMMUNITIES

Biological indicators of water quality include measuring the responses of individuals to a particular stressor at the cellular level, single-species toxicity tests, and the analysis of community or ecosystem structure and function. Stream water quality evaluation has moved away from relying on the indicator organism concept and biotic indices (Cairns and Pratt 1993) and toward rapid bioassessment methods using both multimetric and multivariate tools.

MULTIMETRIC AND MULTIVARIATE APPROACHES

Multimetric and multivariate tools for analyzing macroinvertebrate data are continually being developed and have been widely applied to stream water quality evaluation (Plafkin et al. 1989; Barbour et al. 1996; Reynoldson et al. 1997; Barbour et al. 1999; Karr and Chu 1999; Stribling, Jessup, and Gerritsen 2000).

Multimetric approaches are quite useful because they incorporate information about individuals, populations, communities, and ecosystems, which incorporates individuals into landscapes (Karr and Chu

1999). There are many examples of indices that can be measured from typical macroinvertebrate data collected in monitoring studies. A few examples include measures of individual tolerance, taxa richness, taxa composition, diversity, trophic structure, and life history attributes. Karr and Chu (1999) provide an excellent synthesis of using multimetric methods for evaluating ecological integrity.

Multivariate methods are useful when applied to macroinvertebrate data because these techniques provide ways to describe the multiple variables (e.g., multiple species) often measured during water quality investigations. These methods are commonly used in Europe, Canada, and Australia for assessing water quality (Reynoldson et al. 1995; Simpson et al. 1996) and are becoming accepted in the United States. The application of additional multivariate methods to water quality evaluation are reviewed in Norris and Georges (1993) and Sparks, Scott, and Clarke (1999). Cao and Larsen (2001) provide rare species considerations of multivariate methods. Reynoldson et al. (1997) recommend using a combination of multimetric and multivariate approaches to assess water quality.

THE INDICATOR ORGANISM CONCEPT

Aquatic insects collectively exhibit a wide range of tolerance to environmental conditions. Species or taxonomic groups not occurring under severe ecological conditions are said to be intolerant. Those with a wide range of tolerance, but unable to tolerate severe ecological conditions, are said to be facultative. Species or groups occurring under severe ecological conditions are tolerant. Whereas intolerant organisms do not occur under severe conditions, tolerant organisms may also inhabit pristine waters. One must, of course, specify the ecological conditions of concern (e.g., heavy metals, pH levels, organic pollution, water temperature) because a species may be included in all three categories (intolerant, facultative, tolerant), depending upon which variable is examined. Knowing that an organism is, for example, intolerant of organic pollution does not indicate whether it is low oxygen, high turbidity, sedimentation, or a combination of these and other factors that are responsible for its absence. In addition, many species of aquatic insects have specific requirements relating to substrate type, current velocity, temperature, and other natural variables; their presence or absence may be unrelated to alterations induced by humans, or

they may be indirectly influenced by changes in the food base or com-
petitive and predator-prey interactions. Lists are available that indicate the tolerance levels of specific taxonomic groups of aquatic insects
to particular environmental conditions (Weber 1973; Beck 1977; Harris and Lawrence 1978; Hubbard and Peters 1978; Surdick and Gaufin
1978; United States Department of Agriculture Forest Service 1989;
Barbour et al. 1999).

Unimpacted and impacted stations may be compared simply on the
basis of percentage composition (e.g., percent tolerant, facultative, and
intolerant). A variety of biotic indices have also been developed that
provide a single numerical value based on the organisms present (Hawkes
1979; Lenat 1993). The usefulness of these biotic indices heavily depends on the reliability of the tolerance values assigned to each species
to reflect the type of human disturbance being measured. One of the
simplest is Beck's Biotic Index (BBI) (Beck 1955):

BBI = 2INT + FAC

where INT = the number of intolerant species and FAC = the
number of facultative species.

Because the number of intolerant species is multiplied by two, the index value is highest in clean waters as follows:

BBI = 0—gross organic pollution
BBI = 1 to 6—moderate pollution
BBI = 4 to 9—clean water with moderate or slow current
BBI = 10 to 40—clean water with rapid current

COMMUNITY STRUCTURE

The structure of a biotic community may be described in a variety of
ways. The percentage composition of functional feeding groups in the
community (see Fig. 10) has already been addressed. Frequently, data
on the relative contributions of taxonomic categories are presented in
histograms or pie diagrams. For example, if stoneflies made up 15 percent of the total benthic biomass at one station, but only 1 percent at
a location a short distance downstream, a major habitat alteration at-
tributable to human activities is indicated.

Species diversity has been widely used as an index of potential disturbance in stream communities. Species diversity has two components,

richness (total number of species) and evenness (distribution of individuals among the species). Just as a community of twenty species is more diverse than a community of ten species, so is a community of ten species, each with ten individuals, more diverse than a community of ten species, one of which has ninety-one individuals with the remaining nine species each with a single individual. Diversity is the degree of uncertainty of predicting what species an individual picked at random will be. Uncertainty, and thus diversity, increase both as the number of species increases (richness component) and as the individuals become more evenly distributed among the species (evenness or equitability component). High species diversity characterizes natural communities. Severe water pollution results in low diversity, either through a reduced number of species or by allowing a few species to develop extremely large populations, thereby reducing equitability.

Several indices have been developed to measure species diversity. The Shannon-Weaver index (Shannon and Weaver 1963) has commonly been used to measure diversity in stream macroinvertebrates. The Shannon-Weaver index (abbreviated $\overline{d}$) is predicated upon assumptions that (1) the sample collected is a random sample from an infinitely large population and (2) all species present in the community are represented in the sample. Because both of these assumptions are rarely met, the diversity index should be used with caution and in conjunction with other biotic and abiotic data. In a strict sense, each taxon should be identified to species, which is often an impossible task with aquatic insects. However, it is not necessary to know the species name; recognizing different taxa is all that is needed.

The Shannon-Weaver index may be calculated from the following:

$$\overline{d} = \frac{C}{D} \left(N \log_{10} N - \sum n_i \log_{10} n_i \right)$$

where C = 3.322 (converts base 10 log to base 2),
N = total number of individuals, and
n_i = total number of individuals of the ith species.

The calculations are simple, as is exemplified for the following hypothetical community:

$n_i's$	n_i	$log_{10}n_i$*
species 1	128	269.72
species 2	86	166.37
species 3	18	22.59
species 4	12	12.95
species 5	10	10.00
Totals	254	481.63

*From Table 5 in Weber 1973.

N = 254 (total number of individuals)
s = 5 (total number of species)
$\Sigma n_i \, log_{10} \, n_i$ = 481.63
$\overline{d}$ = 3.322/254 (610.83–481.63) = 1.69

The equitability (e) component of diversity of Lloyd and Ghelardi (1964) is based on the following:

$$e = \frac{s'}{s}$$

where s' = a value from Table 6 in Weber (1973) and s = the number of species. In the preceding example, s = 5 and s' = 4; therefore:

$$e = \frac{4}{5} = 0.8$$

Wilhm (1970) calculated values from aquatic macroinvertebrate data collected by numerous investigators who used a variety of collecting techniques and sampled a diverse array of habitat types. Almost invariably, macroinvertebrate communities of unpolluted waters exhibited $\overline{d}$ values between 3.0 and 4.0, whereas values from polluted streams were generally less than 1.0. However, Weber (1973) feels that $\overline{d}$ lacks the sensitivity to detect slight stream degradation and suggests using equitability (e). In unpolluted streams in the southeastern United States, equitability normally ranges from 0.6 to 0.8, whereas even mild levels of organic wastes generally depress equitability values below 0.3. Most $\overline{d}$ values for Rocky Mountain streams generally approach or exceed 3.0 (Platts, Megahan, and Minshall 1983).

INSECTS of COLORADO MOUNTAIN STREAMS

Several major taxonomic categories of aquatic insects are restricted to running waters, and many other groups attain their maximum abundance and diversity in stream habitats (Hynes 1970a). Although less than 3 percent of all species of insects have aquatic stages (Daly 1996), insects, in terms of numbers, are the most important benthic animals in many stream habitats, often constituting over 90 percent of the total macroinvertebrates in mountain streams.

Thirteen orders of insects contain species with aquatic or semi-aquatic habits (Table 6). All species of Ephemeroptera, Odonata, Plecoptera, Megaloptera, and Trichoptera have aquatic stages (rare exceptions are known, but not among the Colorado fauna). The remaining eight orders are primarily terrestrial groups that contain aquatic or semiaquatic species. Only a very few collembolans are truly aquatic. It is contentious whether they are even insects, and they will not be considered further herein (the interested reader is referred to Waltz and McCafferty 1979). Two orders are not known to have truly aquatic representatives in Colorado, although further investigation is needed. Several

Table 6—The orders of insects containing aquatic or semiaquatic species in North America, their aquatic association, and the known occurrences of aquatic representatives in Colorado.

Order (Common Name)	Aquatic Association	Colorado Lotic	Colorado Lentic
Collembola (springtails)	Primarily terrestrial; some truly aquatic species	+	+
Ephemeroptera (mayflies)	All species aquatic	+	+
Odonata (dragonflies)	All species aquatic	+	+
Hemiptera (true bugs)	Primarily terrestrial; some truly aquatic species	+	+
Orthoptera (grasshoppers, etc.)	Primarily terrestrial; some semiaquatic species	–	–
Plecoptera (stoneflies)	All species aquatic	+	(+)
Coleoptera (beetles)	Primarily terrestrial; some truly aquatic species	+	+
Diptera (true flies)	Primarily terrestrial; some truly aquatic species	+	+
Hymenoptera (bees, ants, etc.)	Primarily terrestrial; some truly aquatic species	–	–
Lepidoptera (moths and butterflies)	Primarily terrestrial; some truly aquatic species	+	+
Megaloptera (dobsonflies, etc.)	All species aquatic	+	+
Neuroptera (lacewings, etc.)	Primarily terrestrial; some truly aquatic species	+	–
Trichoptera (caddisflies)	All species aquatic	+	+

Note: + = present; (+) = a few species occur in cold lakes at high elevation; – = not present or unknown.

families of orthopterans contain semiaquatic species, such as the pygmy mole crickets (Tridactylidae), which are often common along the shores of streams. Adults of some species of Hymenoptera enter the water to parasitize aquatic insects (Hagen 1996), but there are no known occurrences in Colorado waters. Truly aquatic hemipterans are rarely encountered in rapid streams. Only one small family of Neuroptera, the Sisyridae (spongillaflies), contains truly aquatic species. As the name implies, these insects are parasites of freshwater sponges. *Sisyra vicaria* has been collected from several eastern (Great Plains) Colorado streams. Only the underwater stages of the remaining nine orders are treated further here. Water striders (Hemiptera) and other groups residing on the surface film are thus excluded from consideration, and only brief mention is made of the aerial stages of truly aquatic species. Five major groups—stoneflies, mayflies, caddisflies, dipterans, and elmid beetles—typically make up nearly 100 percent of the benthic fauna in Colorado mountain streams. Even these well-represented orders lack families present in adjacent states. Examples include peltoperlid stoneflies, baetiscid mayflies, and psephenid beetles. The near absence of major groups, such as Odonata, from high-gradient mountain streams is also striking. In contrast to the level of research carried out in some other western states, remarkably few detailed analyses have been conducted on the taxonomy, distribution, and biology of specific groups of aquatic insects in Colorado. Much work remains to be done.

KEY TO ORDERS

The following key to orders, and subsequent keys to families and genera, are restricted to insects commonly occurring in Colorado mountain streams. The keys to families and genera are considerably simplified by this restriction. See Merritt and Cummins's (1996) identification keys for the entire North American aquatic insect fauna. Additionally, Voshell (2001) provides a useful illustrated guide to the freshwater invertebrates of North America.

KEY TO THE FREE-LIVING UNDERWATER STAGES OF THE ORDERS OF INSECTS WITH AQUATIC REPRESENTATIVES IN COLORADO MOUNTAIN STREAMS, EXCLUSIVE OF PUPAE

1. Wings or wing pads present, compound eyes usually present (Fig. 15)..2

    Possessing neither wings nor wing pads, compound eyes absent (Figs. 60, 102)...7

2. Fully developed membranous wings present (may be inconspicuous), Adults..3

    Fully developed membranous wings absent, but wing pads present, Nymphs...4

3. First pair of wings hardened to form a shell-like covering (the elytra) over the abdomen (see Fig. 89); the second pair of wings (membranous) is under the elytra; chewing mouthparts...............................
    ....Adult Coleoptera (Beetles) (p. 132)

    First pair of wings with a hardened base and a membranous apical portion (hemelytra); sucking mouthparts, formed as a long jointed beak....................Adult Hemiptera (true bugs) (p. 161)

4. With two or three terminal segmented filaments on abdomen (Figs. 28, 49)..5

    Without terminal segmented filaments on abdomen (unsegmented terminal gills may be present)...6

5. Two claws on each leg; two filaments; without lateral abdominal gills (Fig. 15).....................Nymphal Plecoptera (stoneflies) (p. 55)

    One claw on each leg; two or three filaments; usually with lateral abdominal gills (Fig. 41)..
    ....Nymphal Ephemeroptera (mayflies) (p. 80)

6. Raptorial mouthparts forming a large hinged structure (mask) held under the head (Fig. 110)..
    ....Nymphal Odonata (dragonflies and damselflies) (p. 160)

    Piercing mouthparts forming a long jointed beak.............................
    ....Nymphal Hemiptera (true bugs) (p. 161)

7. With three pairs of jointed legs on thorax (Fig. 78).....................8

    Without jointed legs on thorax (Fig. 96)...
    .... Larval Diptera (true flies) (p. 139)

8. With two or more pairs of abdominal prolegs terminating in a circle of hooklets..................Larval Lepidoptera (aquatic moths) (p. 161)

    Prolegs absent or confined to last abdominal segment (Figs. 78, 111)..9

9. Abdomen with seven or eight pairs of stout lateral processes, arranged one pair per abdominal segment (Fig. 111); final segment with anal hooks or a single caudal filament.....................................
    ....Larval Megaloptera (alderflies and dobsonflies) (p. 160)

    Normally without stout lateral processes on abdomen (fleshy filamentous processes may be present); if stout lateral processes present, then anal hooks are absent or the terminal segment has four gills, or caudal filament is absent or paired (rather than single)...............10

10. With a pair of terminal abdominal prolegs (Fig. 78), often residing in cases...........................Larval Trichoptera (caddisflies) (p. 105)

    Without terminal abdominal prolegs; without cases (Fig. 88)
    ....Larval Coleoptera (beetles) (p. 133)

PLECOPTERA

The Plecoptera (stoneflies), more than any other order of insects, are typical inhabitants of running waters. Nearly all species occur exclusively in streams, and most are restricted to cold lotic habitats (Wiggins and Mackay 1978; Baumann 1979; Stewart and Stark 1988). Colorado mountain streams thus provide ideal stonefly habitat, and all but one of the North American families have been recorded from Colorado (Table 7). Colorado mountain streams contain 72 percent of the genera and 53 percent of the species of the Rocky Mountain stonefly fauna (Baumann, Gaufin, and Surdick 1977). See Kondratieff and Baumann (in press) and Appendix B for the known Colorado distribution of stoneflies.

Most stonefly nymphs are herbivores, feeding principally on plant detritus (Hynes 1976; see references cited in Stewart and Stark 1988). Even the young nymphs of many carnivorous species feed on fine detritus before switching to animal prey. Mature nymphs range in length from a few millimeters (some capniids) to over five centimeters (*Pteronarcys californica*). Although some species emerge in autumn, most stoneflies transform to adults in spring or early summer. Numerous "winter stoneflies" occur in Colorado. These species typically emerge as soon as openings appear in the ice (late winter, early spring); the dark-colored adults are easily seen on snow-covered stream banks.

"The Stoneflies (Plecoptera) of the Rocky Mountains" (Baumann, Gaufin, and Surdick 1977) provides taxonomic keys to nymphs and adults. Additionally, Stewart and Stark (1988) provide keys and diagnoses for all the genera. A wonderful overview of the order is presented by Stark, Szczytko, and Nelson (1998), providing color photographs of many of the nymphs of Colorado mountain stream genera. The web site maintained by B. P. Stark, http:www.mc.edu/~stark/stonefly.html, provides a listing of all North American species by province or state.

Several investigators have examined food habits (Richardson and Gaufin 1971; Fuller and Stewart 1977, 1979; Short and Ward 1981; Allan 1982), predatory behavior (Peckarsky 1980), life history (DeWalt and Stewart 1995; Taylor, Anderson, and Peckarsky 1999; Sandberg and Stewart 2001), and production (Short and Ward 1980c) of Colorado stoneflies. Data on the altitudinal zonation of stoneflies in the Colorado Rocky Mountains have also been presented (Dodds and Hisaw 1925b; Knight and Gaufin 1966; Ward 1982, 1986; Ruse and Herrmann 2000).

Table 7—Known representation of stoneflies (Plecoptera) in Colorado mountain streams.

Order Family	Number of Genera		Number of Species	
Plecoptera	40	(100)	87	(629)
Capniidae	8	(10)	21	(152)
Chloroperlidae	6	(12)	15	(89)
Leuctridae	2	(7)	5	(55)
Nemouridae	5	(12)	12	(71)
Peltoperlidae	0	(6)	0	(20)
Perlidae	4	(15)	4	(74)
Perlodidae	9	(30)	21	(123)
Pteronarcyidae	2	(2)	2	(10)
Taeniopterygidae	4	(6)	7	(35)

Source: Numbers in parentheses, which include both lotic and lentic habitats, are totals for North America adjusted from Stark, Szczytko, and Nelson (1998).

Note: See Appendix B for known distributions of Colorado species by drainage basin.

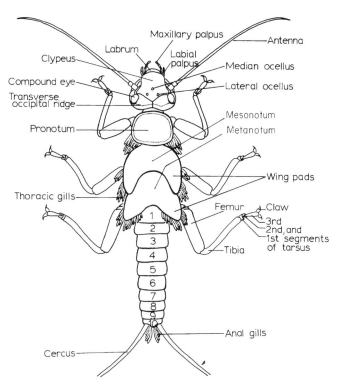

Fig. 15. Morphology of a generalized stonefly nymph. Dorsal view.

A generalized perlid stonefly nymph is used to illustrate the external morphology of aquatic insects in general and hemimetabolous insects in particular (Figs. 15, 16, 17). These figures should be referred to when using the taxonomic keys.

The family key to stoneflies (and other orders) includes all families occurring in Colorado mountain streams. The generic keys, however, include only genera commonly encountered in such habitats in Colorado. By excluding rare genera, those unlikely to be encountered in general collections, it is possible to simplify the keys without greatly sacrificing accuracy. Identification keys for immature stoneflies (and other orders) are based on the characteristics of late instars; it may not be possible to determine the genus of earlier instars. It should be emphasized that taxonomic keys are only guides (normally imperfect guides) to identification. The construction of perfect keys is precluded by normal intraspecific variations, anomalous characteristics, the influence of environmental conditions on key characters, and several other factors. The careful investigator does not rely solely on keys but also consults more complete descriptions in the literature and reference collections of confirmed specimens.

KEY TO COLORADO FAMILIES OF PLECOPTERA NYMPHS

1. Branched gills on ventral side of basal abdominal segments 1–2 or 1–3...Pteronarcyidae (p. 58)

    Without branched gills on ventral side of basal abdominal segments 2

2. Paraglossae and glossae of labium of about equal length (Fig. 18).......3

    Paraglossae much longer than glossae (Figs. 17, 19).......................6

3. Second tarsal segment much shorter than first (Fig. 20)..................4

    Second tarsal segment at least as long as first (Fig. 21)...................
    ....Taeniopterygidae (p. 58)

4. Body stout; axis of hind wing pads strongly divergent from body axis (Fig. 28)..................................Nemouridae (p. 59)

    Body slender; axis of hindwing pads nearly parallel with body axis (Figs. 29, 30)...5

5. Sterna and terga of all abdominal segments separated laterally by a membranous fold (Fig. 22)....................Capniidae (p. 59)

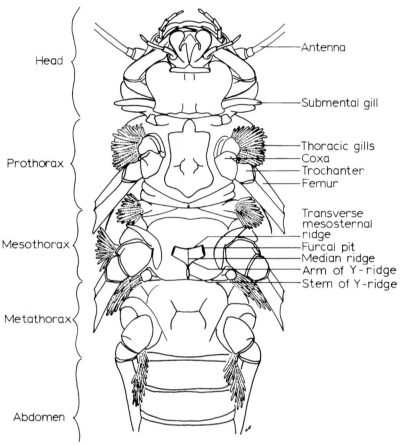

Fig. 16. Morphology of a generalized stonefly nymph. Ventral view excluding most of abdomen.

Only the first seven or fewer abdominal segments divided laterally by a membranous fold; the sterna and terga are fused on the remaining segments, thus forming a continuous ring (Fig. 23); body very elongate (Fig. 30).....................................Leuctridae (p. 61)

6. Branched gills on thorax; apex of paraglossae rounded (Fig. 19)......
    ....Perlidae (p. 62)

    Without branched gills on thorax; apex of paraglossae pointed (Fig. 17)...7

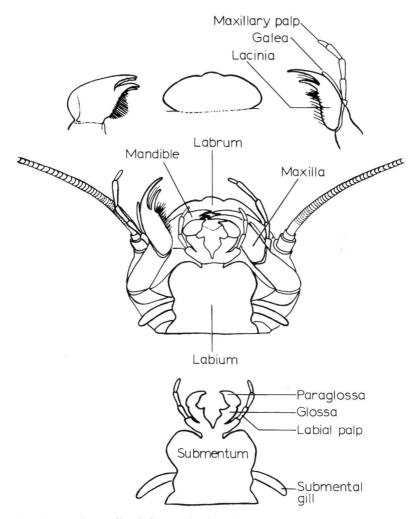

Fig. 17. Ventral view of head of a generalized stonefly nymph showing mouthparts both in situ and separated from the remainder of the head.

7. Terminal segment of maxillary palp much thinner than preceding segment (Fig. 24); axis of hind wing pads nearly parallel to body axis; cerci three-fourths or less length of abdomen............Chloroperlidae (p. 63)

Terminal segment of maxillary palp only slightly thinner than preceding segment (Fig. 17); axis of hind wing pads divergent from body axis; cerci at least as long as abdomen.........Perlodidae (p. 62)

Family Pteronarcyidae. This family is represented in Colorado by two genera that may be distinguished as follows:

1. Branched gills on the ventral side of the first two abdominal segments...*Pteronarcys*

   Branched gills on the ventral side of the first three abdominal segments ....*Pteronarcella*

Baumann, Gaufin, and Surdick (1977) provide keys to the Rocky Mountain species of these genera. In Colorado each of these genera has but a single confirmed species. *Pteronarcys californica* (Fig. 26) is the largest stonefly in Colorado, and is known as the salmonfly to anglers; *Pteronarcella badia* is much smaller. Both are dark-colored stoneflies characteristic of lower-elevation mountain streams in Colorado. They are shredders that typically feed on leaf detritus, and are among the few Colorado mountain stream insects requiring more than one year to complete their life cycles. *Pteronarcys californica* requires three to four years to complete one generation (Townsend and Pritchard 2000). *Pteronarcella badia* is thought to have either a one- or two-year life cycle. Adult emergence typically occurs in May or June for both species.

Family Taeniopterygidae. Four genera of these late winter– and early spring–emerging species have been reported from this family in Colorado. The nymphs may be separated as follows:

1. Fingerlike gills present on coxae (Fig. 25).......................*Taeniopteryx*

   Coxal gills absent...2

2. Cerci with a dense fringe of long setae................................*Doddsia*

   Cerci without a dense fringe of long setae.....................................3

3. A single long seta on basal segment of cerci.....................*Oemopteryx*

   Cerci without a long seta on basal segments.....................*Taenionema*

Taenionema is the most common genus of this family in Colorado, and *T. pallidum* (Fig. 27) is the most common species. See Stanger and Baumann (1993) for a review of *Taenionema*. *Doddsia occidentalis* is a common higher-elevation species, but *Oemopteryx fosketti* is limited to lower-elevation, large, silty rivers and has been reported from only the Yampa and Colorado River basins. *Taeniopteryx* is a primarily eastern genus, with *T. burksi* reported from the North Fork of the Republican River and tributaries (Kondratieff and Ward 1987), and *T. parvula* from the

North Platte River basin (Kondratieff and Baumann 1988). Kondratieff and Baumann (1988) provide a key to the nymphs.

Family Nemouridae. Five genera have been reported from Colorado and may be separated as follows:

1. Cervical (ventral neck region) gills present.............................2
   Cervical gills absent...4
2. Cervical gills with many branches (five or more)........................3
   Four cervical gills simple, or each with no more than four branches..... ....*Zapada*
3. Cervical gill branches all originating at base.................*Amphinemura*
   Some cervical gills branched some distance from base............*Malenka*
4. A fringe of long hairs on outer margin of foretibia...................*Prostoia*
   Without a fringe of long hairs on outer margin of foretibia (a few long hairs may be present)...*Podmosta*

Baumann, Gaufin, and Surdick (1977) provide nymphal keys to some of the Rocky Mountain species of *Zapada*, but adults are usually required for species identification of the members of this family. In Colorado mountain streams, *Zapada* is the most common genus in this family; *Z. cinctipes* and *Z. haysi* (nymphs of *Z. haysi* key to the *Z. oregonensis* group in Baumann, Gaufin, and Surdick [1977]) can be abundant. Only one species of *Prostoia* (*P. besametsa*) occurs in most medium to larger mountain streams in Colorado, and nymphs and adults are present from February to April. The two *Podmosta* species are typically associated with higher-elevation streams. *Amphinemura banksi* and species of *Malenka* also can be common in certain mountain streams. The nymphs of members of this family are characterized by their stout, robust habitus with divergent wing pads and by spines on the legs, thorax, and abdomen (Fig. 28). They are primarily detritivore shredders.

Family Capniidae. Five genera of capniids have been reported from Colorado mountain streams. The nymphs of some species are difficult to identify even at the generic level. The nymphs of the most common genera are separated as follows:

1. A dense fringe of long swimming hairs on the cerci (very rare)......... ....*Isocapnia*
   Cerci lacking dense fringe of long swimming hairs........................2

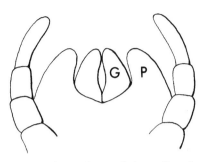

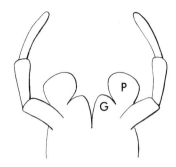

Fig. 18. Labium of a nymphal stonefly with glossae (G) and paraglossae (P) equal.

Fig. 19. Labium of a nymphal stonefly with paraglossae (P) longer than glossae (G).

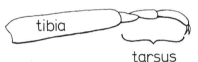

Fig. 20. Tibia and tarsus of a nymphal stonefly with second tarsal segment much shorter than the first segment.

Fig. 21. Tibia and tarsus of a nymphal stonefly with second tarsal segment at least as long as first segment.

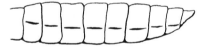

Fig. 22. Lateral view of the abdomen of a nymphal stonefly with the sterna and terga of all abdominal segments separated laterally by a membranous fold.

Fig. 23. Lateral view of the abdomen of a nymphal stonefly with the sterna and terga of only the first seven or fewer abdominal segments separated laterally by a membranous fold.

Fig. 24. The maxillary palp of a nymphal chloroperlid stonefly showing the much thinner terminal segment.

2.　Body and appendages with conspicuous long bristles; often darker coloration between compound eyes (uncommon)..............*Paracapnia*

　　Body and appendages with few bristles, head without distinct coloration...3

3.　Lacinia of maxilla with a single poorly sclerotized cusp; an average of seventeen segments on each cercus............................*Eucapnopsis*

　　Lacinia of maxilla with two or more cusps, an average of twenty-five segments on each cercus...3

3.　Femur and tibia of foreleg with more than fifty fine hairs.....*Utacapnia*

　　Femur and tibia of foreleg with fewer than twenty-five fine hairs.....

　　...*Capnia* and *Capnura*

This family is composed primarily of small species and contains many "winter stoneflies," adults typically emerging from January to April. Twenty species of capniids have been recorded from Colorado mountain streams (Kondratieff and Baumann, in press), eight of which are in the genus *Capnia* (Appendix B). There are no nymphal keys for species identification for this family. However, only one species of *Eucapnopsis* (*E. brevicauda*, Fig. 29) occurs in North America and emerges later than most *Capnia* species. An eastern species, *Paracapnia angulata*, can be abundantly collected from streams of the North Platte basin (Jackson County) and the Poudre River (Larimer County). Nelson and Baumann (1987, 1989) provide keys to adult *Capnura* and *Capnia*, respectively. Not included in the key is the species *Mesocapnia frisoni*, known only from two lower-elevation Colorado locations, the Little Thompson River (Larimer County) and Arkansas River (Pueblo County) (Kondratieff and Baumann, in press; Ruse and Herrmann 2000). Most species of capniids are detritivore shredders.

Family Leuctridae. Only two genera of leuctrids have been reported from Colorado mountain streams; the nymphs may be separated as follows:

1.　Corners of pronotum with four to eight bristles...............*Paraleuctra*

　　Corners of pronotum without bristles..............................*Perlomyia*

The Colorado members of this family are similar to capniids, but leuctrid nymphs are generally more elongate and the abdominal segments are not prominently wider posteriorly as in capniids (Fig. 30).

There are no species keys for the immature leuctrids. *Paraleuctra vershina* is the most common and widespread Colorado species, with an additional three species of the genus recorded from the state (Stark and Kyzar 2000). *Perlomyia utahensis* is the only species of this genus known from Colorado, and has been rarely collected.

Family Perlidae. The nymphs of the three common genera of perlids with confirmed records in Colorado mountain streams are separated as follows:

1. Occiput of head with a complete transverse row of regularly spaced spinules (Fig. 31)..*Claassenia*

    Occiput with only a few spinules or with a sinuate or incomplete row of irregularly spaced spinules..2

2. With only a few spinules scattered on occiput behind eyes.......
    ....*Acroneuria*

    Occiput with a nearly complete, but irregularly spaced, sinuate row of spinules...*Hesperoperla*

Claassenia has only one Nearctic species (*C. sabulosa*, Fig. 31), and *Hesperoperla* is represented in Colorado by a single common species (*H. pacifica*, Fig. 32). *Acroneuria abnormis* is the only confirmed species of that genus that occurs in the Rocky Mountains, recorded from the lower Colorado River drainage (Mesa and Moffat Counties). Another perlid, *Perlesta decipiens* (not included in the key), has been collected from tributaries of the Poudre River, South Platte River, North Fork of Republican River drainage, and Conejos River (Kondratieff and Baumann, in press). The perlids are relatively large and conspicuous stoneflies. The nymphs are predaceous, feeding largely on other aquatic insects. Alexander and Stewart (1996) discuss the fascinating aspects of the adult mating behavior of a Colorado population of *C. sabulosa*.

Family Perlodidae. Nine of the eleven Rocky Mountain genera of perlodids occur in Colorado. Nymphs of the eight common Colorado genera may be distinguished as follows:

1. Gills absent; dorsum of abdomen usually with longitudinal stripe(s) (Fig. 33)..*Isoperla*

    Gills usually present; dorsum of abdomen concolorous or with dark and light bands..2

2. Lacinia of maxilla with only the single terminal spine, lacking secondary spines or hairs on mesal margin..........................*Kogotus*
    Lacinia of maxilla with one or more secondary spines and hairs on mesal margin (Fig. 17)..3

3. Mesosternal ridge pattern with a median fork extending to transverse ridge (Fig. 16)..*Isogenoides*
    Mesosternal ridge pattern without median fork 4

4. Y arms of mesosternal ridge pattern meet or approach anterior corners of furcal pits..5
    Y arms of mesosternal ridge pattern meet or approach posterior corners of furcal pits (Fig. 16)..6

5. Three pairs of simple thumblike thoracic gills.....................*Megarcys*
    Thoracic gills absent...*Skwala*

6. Submental gills present, but short...........................*Pictetiella*
    Submental gills absent 7

7. Anterolateral prothoracic margin and occiput with a row of short, stout setae (Fig. 35); inner margin of lacinia with a low knob below subapical tooth...*Diura*
    Anterolateral prothoracic margin and occiput without a row of short, stout setae; inner margin of lacinia without a low knob below subapical tooth...*Cultus*

Szczytko and Stewart (1979) provide keys to *Isoperla* nymphs, at least seven species of which occur in Colorado mountain streams. Baumann, Gaufin, and Surdick (1977) provide keys to the species of *Isogenoides*. Five genera are represented by a single species in Colorado (*Megarcys signata*, Fig. 34; *Diura knowltoni*, Fig. 35; *Pictetiella expansa*; *Skwala americana*; *Kogotus modestus*). Reliable species keys are unavailable for nymphal stages of *Cultus*. Perlodids are medium-sized to moderately large, primarily predaceous stoneflies. If gills are present, they are simple (unbranched) and are restricted to the thorax or submentum in Colorado species.

Family Chloroperlidae. Mature nymphs of the six chloroperlid genera occurring in Colorado are distinguished as follows:

1. Eyes small and set far forward on head; body very elongate (Fig. 36) ....*Paraperla*

Eyes large, not set far forward; body less elongate (Fig. 37)...............2

2. Lacinia of maxilla terminating in a large single tooth; marginal hairs of pronotum sparsely clustered or single and restricted to corners; numerous intrasegmental hairs on cerci......................*Alloperla*

    Lacinia of maxilla terminating in a single large and a single small tooth; marginal hairs of pronotum numerous at least on anterior and posterior margins; intrasegmental hairs absent from cerci.........3

3. Thick, depressed black hairs laterally on all thoracic sterna......*Sweltsa*

    Thick, depressed black hairs absent from lateral thoracic sterna; hairs erect and light-colored..4

4. Marginal hair fringe of pronotum sparse or absent laterally, not uniform; short hair fringe on posterior margins of abdominal terga not regular or uniform; long fine hairs of cerci shorter than cercal segments; abdomen concolorous or with pale longitudinal median stripe, but not checkered..*Suwallia*

    Marginal hair fringe of pronotum thick, regular, uniform, nearly complete or sparse only on lateral margins; short hair fringe on posterior margins of abdominal terga uniform and thick; long fine hairs of cerci longer than cercal segments; abdomen nearly concolorous or with pale checkered pattern....................................5

5. Abdomen distinctly patterned; pronotal hair fringe regular and nearly complete; inner margins of wing pads widely oblique.............*Triznaka*

    Abdomen generally concolorous; pronotal hair fringe sparse laterally; inner margins of wing pads slightly oblique ....*Plumiperla*

The preceding key is based on the revision of Chloroperlinae by Surdick (1985) in which the genus *Plumiperla* was erected for *P. diversa* (formerly *Triznaka diversa*). Generic designations are difficult to ascertain for some species and the key should be used only with late instars. Species keys are unavailable for immature chloroperlids, although the adult color pattern that develops on very mature larvae (e.g., Fig. 37) provides additional key characters. Two genera of chloroperlids are represented in Colorado by a single species (*Paraperla frontalis, Plumiperla diversa*), but other genera contain at least two species (see Appendix B). Alexander and Stewart (1999) revised the genus *Suwallia*, presenting several significant taxonomic changes. Chloroperlids are small, generally elongate stoneflies that lack gills. Nymphs of this family typically inhabit the hyporheic habitat, the interstitial spaces between substrate particles in the streambed. Some species reside at considerable depths in the substrate (Stanford and Ward 1988) and laterally under the banks; therefore, they may be underrepresented by normal sampling techniques. *Paraperla frontalis* is a collector-gatherer and scraper. Other genera are predaceous on other aquatic insects (often chironomids), but also act as collector-gatherers.

Fig. 25. Fingerlike gill on coxae of *Taeniopteryx* (Plecoptera: Taeniopterygidae).

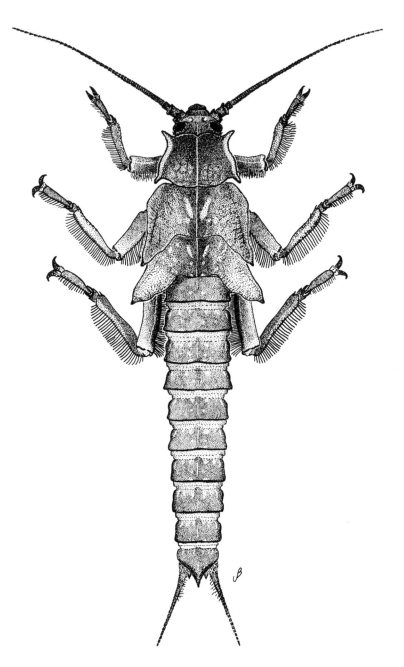

Fig. 26. Dorsal view of a *Pteronarcys californica* nymph (Plecoptera: Pteronarcyidae) (45 mm).

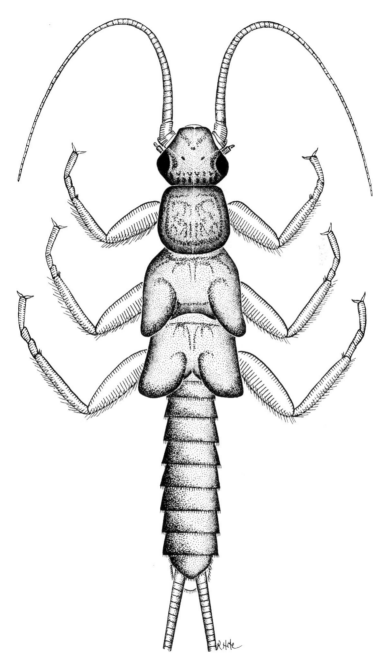

Fig. 27. Dorsal view of a *Taenionema pallidum* nymph (Plecoptera: Taeniopterygidae) (7 mm).

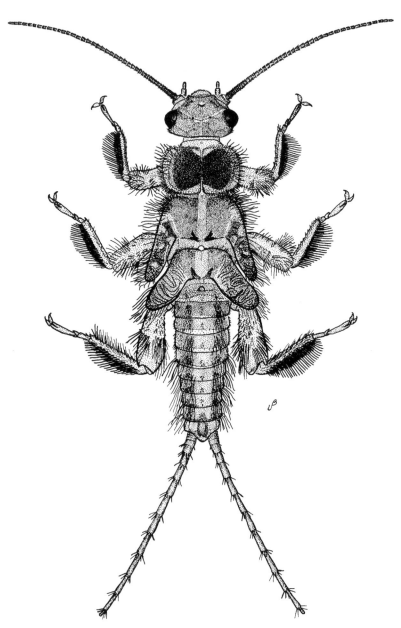

Fig. 28. Dorsal view of a *Zapada oregonensis* nymph (Plecoptera: Nemouridae) (6 mm).

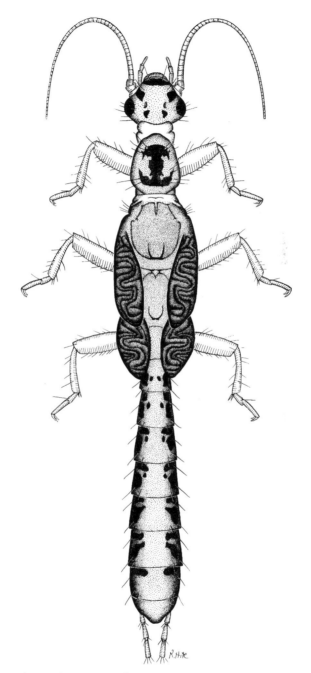

Fig. 29. Dorsal view of a *Eucapnopsis brevicauda* nymph (Plecoptera: Capniidae) (6 mm).

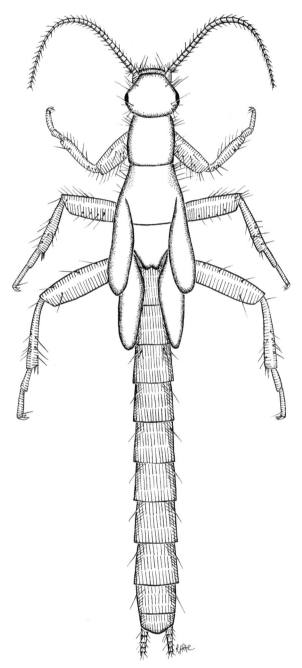

Fig. 30. Dorsal view of a *Paraleuctra occidentalis* nymph (Plecoptera: Leuctridae) (9 mm).

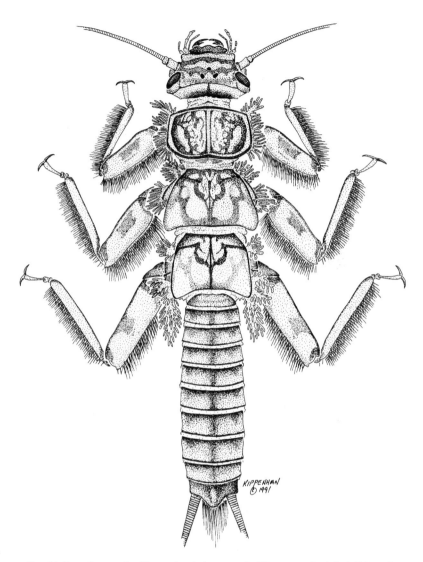

Fig. 31. Dorsal view of a *Claassenia sabulosa* nymph (Plecoptera: Perlidae) (30 mm).

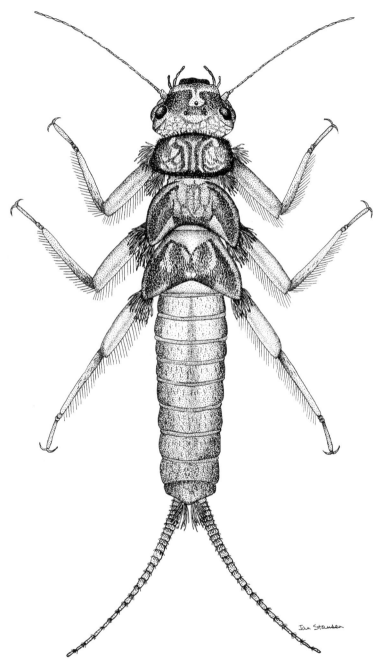

Fig. 32. Dorsal view of a *Hesperoperla pacifica* nymph (Plecoptera: Perlidae) (31 mm).

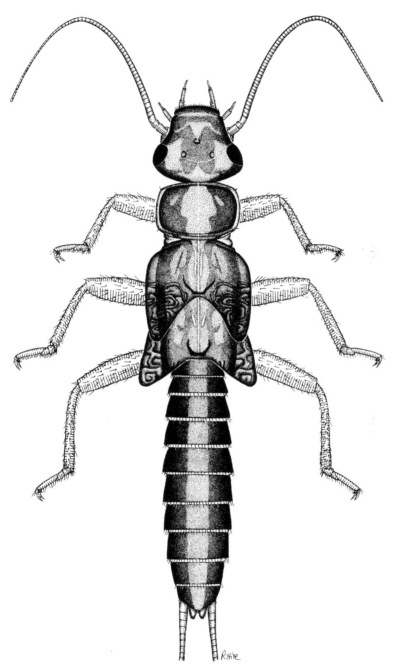

Fig. 33. Dorsal view of an *Isoperla fulva* nymph (Plecoptera: Perlodidae) (11 mm).

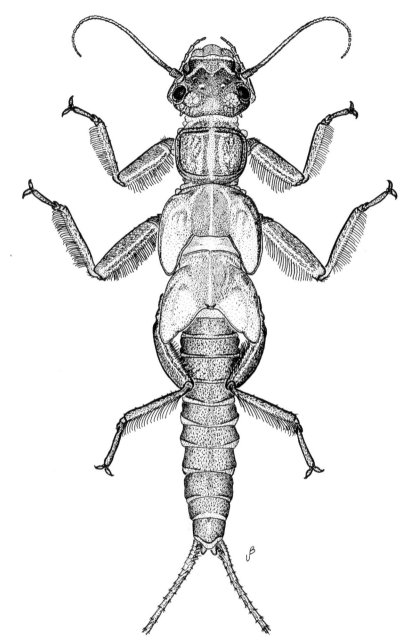

Fig. 34. Dorsal view of a *Megarcys signata* nymph (Plecoptera: Perlodidae) (22 mm).

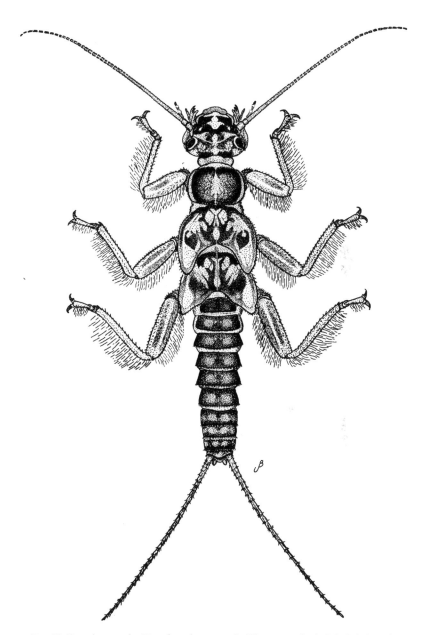

Fig. 35. Dorsal view of a *Diura knowltoni* nymph (Plecoptera: Perlodidae) (15 mm).

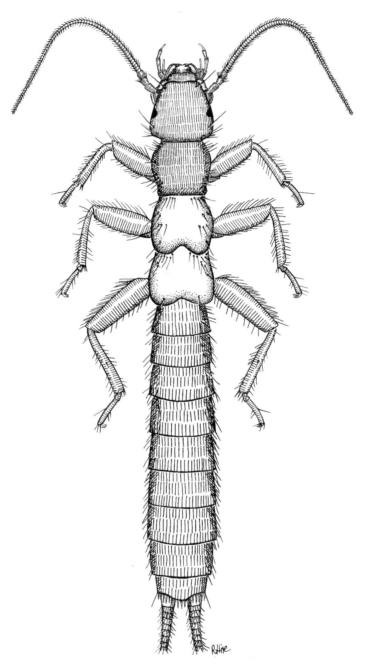

Fig. 36. Dorsal view of a Chloroperlidae (17 mm).

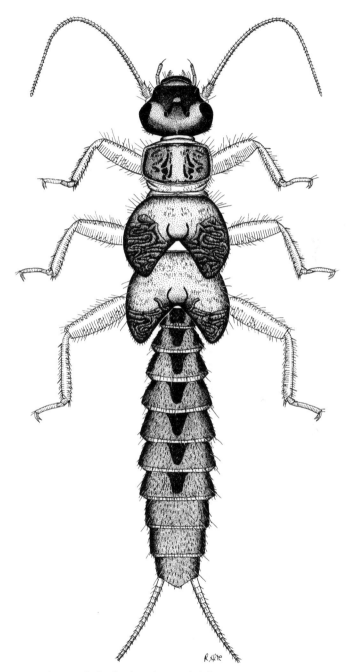

Fig. 37. Dorsal view of a *Sweltsa borealis* nymph (Plecoptera: Chloroperlidae) (15 mm).

EPHEMEROPTERA

The majority of Ephemeroptera (mayflies) reside in running waters, but unlike stoneflies, they attain maximum diversity in warm lotic habitats (Wiggins and Mackay 1978). Colorado mountain streams contain diverse assemblages of eurythermal and cold stenothermal mayflies (Dodds 1923; Ward and Berner 1980; McCafferty, Durfee, and Kondratieff 1993). Six of the nineteen North American families of Ephemeroptera have not been recorded in Colorado mountain streams (Table 8). The missing families are all minor groups in terms of numbers of genera and species. See Appendix A for the known Colorado distribution of lotic mayflies.

Most mayfly nymphs are collector-gatherers or scrapers. A few species are specialized filter-feeders or carnivores. Shredders are very poorly represented. Most mayflies of temperate regions have a one-year life cycle (univoltine), the vast majority of which is spent as an aquatic nymph. In fact, it is the ephemeral nature of the aerial adult stage that is responsible for the Greek name of the order. Adults live from one hour to several days, depending on weather conditions and the species in question.

Edmunds, Jensen, and Berner (1976) provide generic keys and distributional data for the North American mayfly fauna, and Brittain (1982) reviewed the biology of Ephemeroptera. Jensen's (1966) major work on the mayflies of Idaho is still a valuable reference for those studying the Colorado fauna. McCafferty, Durfee, and Kondratieff (1993) listed fourteen families, and ninety-seven species of mayflies from Colorado. Durfee and Kondratieff (1994) added four additional species. More recent keys and taxonomic revisions of specific groups are cited in this book in the discussion of individual families. Although several studies of Colorado mountain streams contain some ecological data on Ephemeroptera, few investigators have dealt specifically with mayflies (Dodds and Hisaw 1924; Ward and Berner 1980; Rader and Ward 1987b, 1989; Ward and Stanford 1990; Ward and Garcia de Jalon 1991; DeWalt et al. 1994). Much work remains to be done.

The general nymphal morphology conforms to that of stoneflies already discussed and illustrated (see Figs. 15–17). The metanotum and second pair of wing pads (when present) are concealed beneath the mesonotum, giving the appearance of only two thoracic segments and a single pair of wing pads (see, e.g., Fig. 40a). The gills of mayflies are

Table 8—Known representation of mayflies (Ephemeroptera) in Colorado mountain streams.

Order Family	Number of Genera		Number of Species	
EPHEMEROPTERA	39	(83)	81	(601)
Acanthametropodidae	0	(2)	0	(2)
Ameletidae	1	(1)	6	(34)
Ametropodidae	1	(1)	1	(3)
Baetidae	12	(22)	21	(133)
Baetiscidae	0	(1)	0	(11)
Behningiidae	0	(1)	0	(1)
Caenidae	2	(4)	5	(24)
Ephemerellidae	5	(8)	10	(85)
Ephemeridae	1	(4)	1	(13)
Heptageniidae	6	(14)	18	(127)
Isonychiidae	1	(1)	2	(16)
Leptohyphidae	2	(2)	3	(25)
Leptophlebiidae	5	(9)	11	(73)
Metretopodidae	0	(2)	0	(9)
Neoephemeridae	0	(1)	0	(4)
Oligoneuriidae	1	(2)	1	(6)
Polymitarcyidae	1	(3)	1	(6)
Potamanthidae	0	(1)	0	(4)
Siphlonuridae	1	(4)	1	(25)

Source: Numbers in parentheses, which include both lotic and lentic habitats, are totals for North America from <http://www.entm.purdue.edu/entomology/mayfly/mayfly/species.html>. The Pseudironidae and Arthropleidae are considered within the Heptageniidae.

Note: See Appendix A for known distributions of Colorado species by major drainage basin.

highly variable. In most species, gills are present only on the abdomen. Gills often occur on the first seven abdominal segments, although one or more pairs may be absent, depending on the species. A very few species also possess gills on the legs and head. Most mayflies possess three caudal filaments; a few have two caudal filaments. Microhabitat occurrence is reflected more distinctly in the morphology of nymphs than in that of any other order. Some species have a fusiform body shape that enables them to move about on the tops of rocks in rapid water (Fig. 49), whereas others are flattened dorsoventrally to hug rock surfaces (Fig. 45). Other groups construct burrows in the substrate with their mandibles and use their gills to create respiratory and feeding currents (Fig. 38). Yet others are adapted for creeping and climbing among accumulations of detritus or in silty backwaters or in plant beds (Fig. 39).

Several approaches to the higher classification of the Ephemeroptera have been offered by Edmunds (1962), McCafferty and Edmunds (1979), and Hubbard (1990). Recently, McCafferty (1991, 1997), and McCafferty and Wang (2000) presented revised phylogenetic arrangements for mayflies. The reader is urged to consult these articles for explanations of mayfly phylogenetic classifications. McCafferty (1996) presents a comprehensive index to North American mayfly species, and his website, http://www.entm.purdue.edu/entomology/mayfly/mayfly/species.html, provides updates of continuing taxonomic changes.

KEY TO COLORADO FAMILIES OF EPHEMEROPTERA NYMPHS

1. Mandibles with large tusks (Fig. 38)..2

    Mandibles without tusks...4

2. Gills without fringed margins...
    ....Leptophlebiidae (*Paraleptophlebia* in part) (p. 85)

    Gill margins fringed (Fig. 38)...3

3. Mandibular tusks curved upward in lateral view........Ephemeridae (p. 81)

    Mandibular tusks curved downward (Fig. 38)........Polymitarcyidae (p. 82)

4. Forelegs with conspicuous fringes of very long hairs....................5

    Forelegs without conspicuous hair fringes..................................6

5. Three caudal filaments; gill tufts present at bases of forecoxae
    ....Isonychiidae (p. 82)

    Two caudal filaments; gill tufts absent from bases of forecoxae
    ....Oligoneuriidae (p. 82)

6. Gills of second abdominal segment operculate, covering succeeding
    pairs (Fig. 39)..7

    Gills of second abdominal segment similar to succeeding gills, or
    absent...8

7. Operculate gills triangular or oval; succeeding gills without fringed
    margins (Fig. 39)...Leptohyphidae (p. 82)

    Operculate gills quadrate; succeeding gills with fringed margins......
    ....Caenidae (p. 83)

8. Gills absent from second abdominal segment........Ephemerellidae (p. 83)

    Gills present on second abdominal segment....................................9

9. Nymphs dorsoventrally flattened; eyes and antennae positioned on top of head (Fig. 45)...10

    Nymphs not flattened dorsoventrally; eyes and antennae positioned laterally on head (Fig. 49)..11

10. Gills of a single flattened plate, usually with a tuft of fibrils at base (Fig. 43a)..Heptageniidae (p. 84)

    Gills of another structure.............Leptophlebiidae (in part) (p. 85)

11. Claws of middle and hind legs very long......Ametropodidae (p. 85)

    Claws short on all legs..12

12. Labrum as broad as or broader than the width of head...................
    ....Leptophlebiidae (in part, *Traverella*) (p. 85)

    Labrum narrower than width of head.......................................13

13. Gills forked (Fig. 47) or consisting of a cluster of filaments or of double plates pointed at the tip...............Leptophlebiidae (in part) (p. 85)

    Gills single or double plates not as above...................................14

14. Median terminal filament highly reduced (two-tailed), or if developed (three-tailed), the antennae are longer than twice the width of the head (Fig. 49)...Baetidae (p. 86)

    Median terminal filament well developed (three-tailed), and antennae shorter than twice the width of the head (Fig. 56).............15

15. Maxillae with crown of pectinate spines (Fig. 55); all gills single plates ....Ameletidae (p. 88)

    Maxillae without pectinate spines; gills on abdominal segments 1–2 subtriangular (Fig. 56)....................................Siphlonuridae (p. 88)

Family Ephemeridae. Only one species from this family of large burrowing mayflies is known to occur in Colorado mountain streams. *Ephemera simulans* has been collected from the White and Yampa Rivers in northwestern Colorado, and Grizzly Creek in Jackson County. Nymphs of this primarily carnivorous species inhabit both running and standing waters. McCafferty (1975) provides species keys and distributional data for all the burrowing mayflies of the United States. McCafferty (1994) provides additional distribution information. *Hexagenia limbata*, a common species of eastern Colorado streams and lakes, has been introduced into several Colorado mountain reservoirs. A burrowing mayfly species, *Ephemera compar*, originally described from the Colorado foothills, is considered extinct (Edmunds and McCafferty 1984).

Family Polymitarcyidae. This family of burrowing mayflies is likewise represented by a single species in Colorado mountain streams. *Ephoron album* (Fig. 38) has been collected from the Poudre, White, Yampa, and Colorado Rivers. Nymphs reside in U-shaped burrows. They feed by filtering organic matter carried through the burrow in the current created by gill movements. Nymphs may also leave their burrows and forage on the substrate surface.

Family Isonychiidae. Two species of this family are known from Colorado, *Isonychia campestris* and *I. rufa*. Members of this family typically reside in riverine habitats. *Isonychia campestris* has been collected from the Colorado River (Mesa County), Douglas Creek (Rio Blanco County), and the lower Yampa River (Moffat County). Another species, *I. rufa*, is known from several Great Plains streams of Front Range and eastern Colorado (Kondratieff and Ward 1987). This species is also known from the lower Arkansas and Purgatoire Rivers of southeastern Colorado. Hair fringes on the forelegs are used to filter organic particles from the water column. Kondratieff and Voshell (1984) provide keys for *Isonychia*.

Family Oligoneuriidae. *Lachlania saskatchewanensis* (= *L. powelli*) are often collected from submerged sticks in rapids of sandy stretches of the Green, Yampa, and White Rivers. Koss and Edmunds (1970) present a key to the three species known in the United States. Durfee and Kondratieff (1994) reported *Homoeoneuria alleni* from near the confluence of the Yampa and Green Rivers in Dinosaur National Monument. Pescador and Peters (1980) provide a key to *Homoeoneuria* nymphs.

Family Leptohyphidae. The two genera reported from Colorado can be distinguished as follows:

1. Body dorsoventrally flattened; forefemora greatly expanded......
   ....*Asioplax*

   Body not dorsoventrally flattened; femora not expanded (Fig. 39)....
   ....*Tricorythodes*

Wiersema and McCafferty (2000) established the generic concepts for this family, two genera of which occur in Colorado. A single variable and common species of *Tricorythodes*, *T. minutus* (Fig. 39), is known to occur in Colorado mountain streams. Nymphs are often associated with beds of aquatic plants or other habitats where silt accumulates. The opercular gills protect the remaining gills from silt deposition. The records of *Asioplax corpulentus* in Colorado suggest that this species is restricted to lower Western Slope riverine habitats. Additionally, another species, *A. edmundsi*, occurs in the Green and Yampa River drainages of western Colorado. Members of this genus are slow-moving sprawlers that feed on sedimentary detritus (collector-gatherers). Allen (1977) provides species keys to known nymphs of *Tricorythodes* and *Asioplax*.

Family Caenidae. Both North American genera of caenids have been reported from Colorado mountain streams. Nymphs are separated as follows:

1. Head with three prominent tubercles; maxillary and labial palpi of two segments..*Brachycercus*

   Head without tubercles; maxillary and labial palpi of three segments..*Caenis*

Caenis more commonly occurs in lentic than in lotic habitats and is uncommonly collected from Colorado mountain streams. Provonsha (1990) provides species keys for *Caenis* adults and nymphs. *Brachycercus*, though primarily an inhabitant of silty streams, has been reported from the upper Colorado River (Soldan 1986).

Family Ephemerellidae. Previously assigned to a single genus (*Ephemerella*), the North American members of this family were placed within eight genera (Allen 1980). Nymphs of the five genera that occur in Colorado are distinguished as follows:

1. Gills present on abdominal segments 3–7 2

   Gills present on abdominal segments 4–7 4

2. Distinct tubercles present on leading edge of swollen forefemora (Fig. 40a); if absent, head, thorax, and abdomen with distinct paired dorsal spines (Fig. 41) ....*Drunella*

   Distinct tubercles absent on leading edge of forefemora; paired dorsal spines lacking on either head, thorax, or abdomen................3

3.   Terminal filaments with whorls of spines on posterior margins of cercal segments and with only sparse intersegmental setae or none; maxillary palpi absent or reduced in size.............................*Serratella*

Terminal filaments with or without whorls of spines on posterior margins of cercal segments and with heavy intersegmental setae; maxillary palpi well developed...*Ephemerella*

4.   Gills on abdominal segment 4 semioperculate; nymph very broad and flat (Fig. 42)...*Timpanoga*

Gills otherwise; nymph not greatly flattened......................*Attenella*

Allen and Edmunds (1959 et seq.) provide keys to the North American species of ephemerellids. *Ephemerella inermis* and *E. infrequens* are very similar but mature nymphs can be separated by characteristics presented by Johnson (1978). This large and diverse family is well represented in Colorado mountain streams. Its members occur from steep gradient segments at high elevations (e.g., *Drunella coloradensis*) to silty microhabitats at lower reaches (e.g., *Timpanoga hecuba*). Most species are considered collector-gatherers or scrapers, but some *Drunella* species, such as *D. doddsi* (Fig. 40a) and *D. grandis* (Fig. 41), have been reported to be partially predaceous.

Family Heptageniidae. Nymphs of the six genera of heptageniids occurring in Colorado are distinguished as follows:

1.   Median caudal filament rudimentary or absent (two-tailed) (Fig. 45)...*Epeorus*

Three well-developed caudal filaments (three-tailed) (Fig. 44).........2

2.   Gills enlarged on abdominal segments 1 and 7 to form ventral oval-shaped disc (Fig. 43b)....................................*Rhithrogena*

First and seventh gills usually smaller than intermediate pairs, do not meet to form a ventral disc.......................................3

3.   Front of head distinctly emarginate medially (Fig. 44); maxillary palpi partially visible at margin of head from dorsal view; fibrils absent from base of gill plates or reduced to one or a few tiny filaments...*Cinygmula*

Front of head without median concave indentation; maxillary palpi not visible from dorsal view; tufts of fibrils at base of gill plates distinct on at least first six pairs of gills (may not be visible dorsally as in Fig. 43a)..4

4. Gill plate on segment 7 with tuft of fibrils; claws with one basal tooth..*Heptagenia*

    Gill plate on segment 7 without tuft of fibrils; claws with small teeth...5

5. Terminal filaments with whorls of spines at articulations; intersegmental setae absent..*Leucrocuta*

    Terminal filaments with intersegmental setae in addition to whorls of spines...*Nixe*

Nymphal keys to species are available for *Epeorus* (Edmunds and Allen 1964); *Heptagenia*, including species now placed in *Leucrocuta* and *Nixe* (Bednarik and Edmunds 1980); and *Rhithrogena* (Jensen 1966). Heptageniids are perhaps the most typically lotic of all mayfly families. The nymphs are dorsoventrally flattened (e.g., Fig. 45) and generally adapted to life in high-gradient mountain streams. Most species are restricted to running waters; a few also inhabit wave-swept shores. Species of *Heptagenia* generally occupy warmer and siltier running waters than other genera. The predaceous heptageniid species *Pseudiron centralis* (often included in the Pseudironidae, but not included in the above key) has been collected from the Green River of northwestern Colorado and the lower Arkansas River in eastern Colorado. Most heptageniids are scrapers; a few are collector-gatherers.

Family Ametropodidae. Ametropus albrighti is the only species of this small family to occur in Colorado. Nymphs are adapted to sand-bottomed riverine environments. The long claws may be used by the nymphs to bury themselves in the sand. Algae associated with the sand appear to be the main food. This species is known only from the Yampa, White, and Little Snake Rivers.

Family Leptophlebiidae. Nymphs of the four genera of leptophlebiids of Colorado mountain streams may be separated as follows:

1. Large mandibular tusks...............................*Paraleptophlebia* (in part)

    Without large mandibular tusks 2

2. Labrum as broad or broader than width of head capsule (Fig. 46).....
    ....*Traverella*

Labrum narrower than width of head capsule..............................3

3. Gills on first abdominal segment similar in structure to those on succeeding segments, may be smaller or more slender; abdominal gills forked (Fig. 47)..............................*Paraleptophlebia* (in part)

    Gills on first abdominal segment different in structure from those on succeeding segments..4

4. Gills on first abdominal segment unforked; succeeding gills are double plates terminating in pointed filaments, the anterior (dorsal) plate with a flattened filament..............................*Choroterpes*

    Gills on first abdominal segment forked; succeeding gills are double plates each terminating in a pointed, slender, unflattened filament.....
    ....*Leptophlebia*

Allen (1973) provides a nymphal key for fourteen species of *Traverella* (only *T. albertana* occurs in Colorado), and Jensen (1966) has a species key for nymphs of some species of *Paraleptophlebia*. Nymphs of two Colorado species of *Paraleptophlebia*, *P. bicornuta* and *P. packi*, possess mandibular tusks. Burian (2001) revised the species of North America, and only recognized *L. cupida* and *L. nebulosa* from Colorado, providing keys to all stages. There are no species keys for nymphs of *Choroterpes*. *Neochoroterpes oklahoma* (= *N. mexicanus*), a species common in the Purgatoire River of southeastern Colorado, has the first gill asymmetrically forked and will not key in the above treatment (Henry 1993). *Traverella albertana* is an abundant filter-feeder in rapid sections of large Western Slope rivers. *Choroterpes* and *Leptophlebia* generally occur in the slower reaches of streams. In small mountain streams, *Paraleptophlebia* is often the only representative of this family. Members of this genus are collector-gatherers and scrapers.

Family Baetidae. Nymphs of the ten common genera of baetids known to occur in Colorado may be distinguished as follows:

1. Claws pointed (Fig. 49)..2

    Claws spatulate, with large teeth along broad, flat apical margin (Fig. 48)..*Camelobaetidius*

2. Basal portion of cerci with narrow dark band at apex of every third to fifth segment..............................*Centroptilum/Procloeon*

    Banding absent from cerci, or with banding pattern other than above 3

3. One or more pairs of gills with recurved posterior (ventral) flap (Fig. 54)..*Callibaetis*

 All gills consist of flat plates without recurved flaps........................4

4. One or both mandibles with a tuft of setae between incisors and prosthecae (Fig. 50)..10

 Both mandibles without a tuft of setae between incisors and prosthecae...5

5. Antennal scapes with a distal notch (Fig. 51) ....*Pseudocloeon*

 Antennal scapes without distal notch (Fig. 49).......................6

6. Middle caudal filament present (Fig. 49); hind wing pads present ....*Baetis* (in part)

 Middle caudal filament reduced or apparently absent; hind wing pads present or absent...7

7. Hind wing pads absent...8

 Hind wing pads present 9

8. Femora, tibiae, and tarsi with row of long setae (Fig. 52)..................
 ....*Acentrella* (in part)

 Femora, tibiae, and tarsi without row of long setae..............*Plauditus*

9. Labial palp segment with well-developed distomedial thumb (Fig. 53)..*Baetis* (in part)

 Labial palp segment without well-developed distomedial thumb ....*Acentrella* (in part)

10. Gill 7 slender and pointed.................................*Acerpenna*

 Gill 7 not slender and pointed....................................11

11. Gills absent on abdominal segment 1, present on 2–7............*Diphetor*

 Gills present on abdominal segments 1–7; pattern on pronotum resembling a pair of eyes; right mandible with a tuft of hairs between prosthecae and molars (Fig. 50) ....*Fallceon*

 The above key incorporates the recent taxonomic changes proposed by Lugo-Ortiz and McCafferty (1998) and Lugo-Ortiz, McCafferty, and Waltz (1999). Other changes are noted in McCafferty and Waltz (1990) and Waltz and McCafferty (1987a and b). Morihara and McCafferty

(1979) provide keys that distinguish the three common Colorado mountain stream *Baetis* species, *B. bicaudatus*, *B. flavistriga*, and *B. tricaudatus*, and *D. hageni* (as *B. hageni*) and *F. quilleri* (as *B. quilleri*). Durfee and Kondratieff (1999) considered *B. moffatti* a synonym of *B. tricaudatus*. The key in McCafferty, Wigle, and Waltz (1994) allows the separation of the nymphs of two Colorado *Acentrella* species, *A. insignificans* and *A. turbida*, whereas McCafferty and Randolph (2000) will key out the two Colorado species of *Camelobaetidius*, *C. kickapoo and C. warreni*. *Camelobaetidius warreni* is an abundant species of the Yampa River in Dinosaur National Monument. The nymphs of the three species of Colorado *Pseudocloeon* (= *Labiobaetis*) can be determined using McCafferty and Waltz (1995). The various species of *Centroptilum* and *Procloeon* are difficult to distinguish without comparative material and original descriptions.

The species of *Baetis* collectively occupy an extremely wide range of lotic habitats. They may be the only mayflies present in extreme environments such as high-elevation streams, the sources of springs, or mildly polluted waters. Often they are, in terms of numbers, the most important mayflies of Colorado mountain streams. *Callibaetis* is primarily a lentic genus, some species of which occur in the backwaters or quiet margins of running waters. *Acentrella* is relatively common, but *Centroptilum/Procloeon*, *Camelobaetidius*, *Plauditus*, and *Pseudocloeon* are rarely collected from Colorado mountain streams. *Heterocloeon frivolum* has been collected occasionally from the North Platte River, Jackson County. Most members of the family are collector-gatherers and scrapers.

Family Ameletidae. *Ameletus* is a common genus in rapid sections of Colorado mountain streams. Nymphs are scrapers, using the pectinate comb of spines (the "diatom rake") on the maxilla (Fig. 55) to feed on periphyton. Zloty (1996) revised the North American species. No keys are currently available to separate the nymphs of Colorado species of *Ameletus*.

Family Siphlonuridae. Jensen (1966) provides nymphal keys to species of *Siphlonurus*, including the most common Colorado species, *S. occidentalis*. Nymphs of this family are generally streamlined forms (Fig. 56) capable of swimming rapidly for short distances. Nymphs of *Siphlonurus* may occur in pools or along the quiet edges of streams but do not occur in high-gradient mountain streams.

Fig. 38. Lateral view of a *Ephoron album* nymph (Ephemeroptera: Polymitarcyidae) (15 mm) (arrow indicates mandibular tusks).

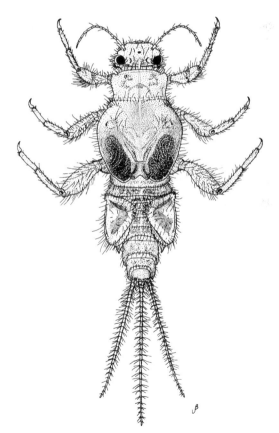

Fig. 39. Dorsal view of a *Tricorythodes minutus* nymph (Ephemeroptera: Leptohyphidae) (7 mm).

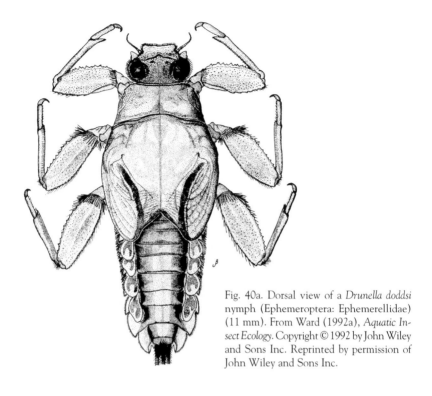

Fig. 40a. Dorsal view of a *Drunella doddsi* nymph (Ephemeroptera: Ephemerellidae) (11 mm). From Ward (1992a), *Aquatic Insect Ecology*. Copyright © 1992 by John Wiley and Sons Inc. Reprinted by permission of John Wiley and Sons Inc.

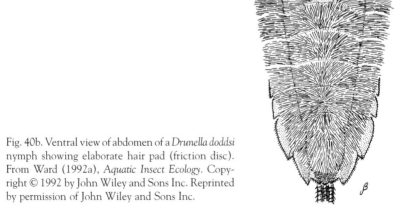

Fig. 40b. Ventral view of abdomen of a *Drunella doddsi* nymph showing elaborate hair pad (friction disc). From Ward (1992a), *Aquatic Insect Ecology*. Copyright © 1992 by John Wiley and Sons Inc. Reprinted by permission of John Wiley and Sons Inc.

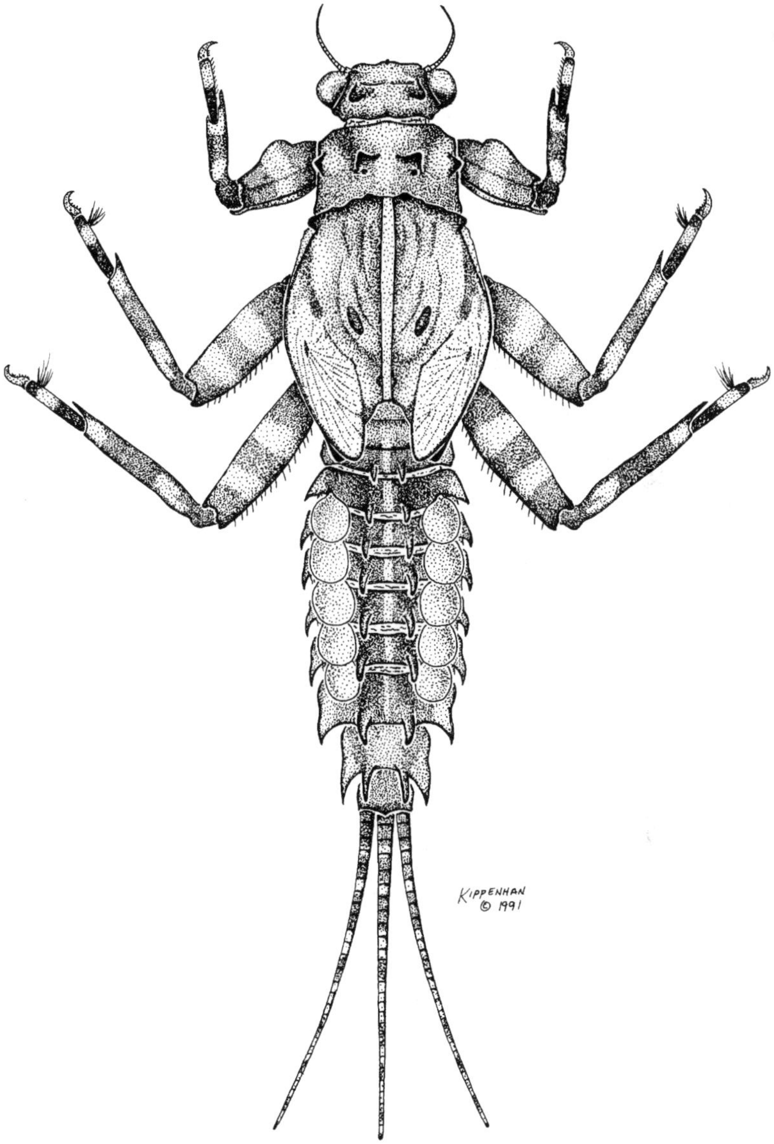

Fig. 41. Dorsal view of a *Drunella grandis* nymph (Ephemeroptera: Ephemerellidae) (14 mm).

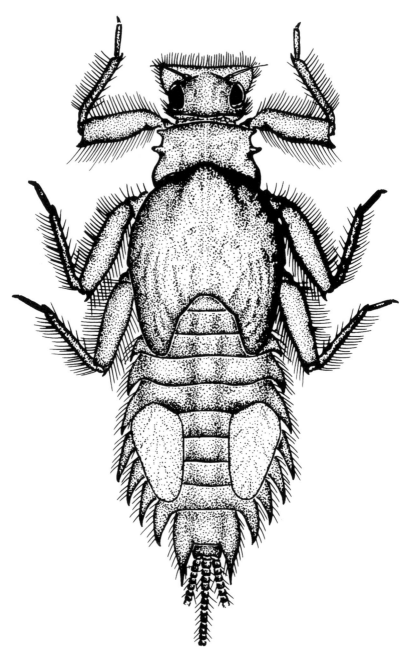

Fig. 42. Dorsal view of *Timpanoga hecuba*. (Ephemeroptera: Ephemerellidae) (16 mm).

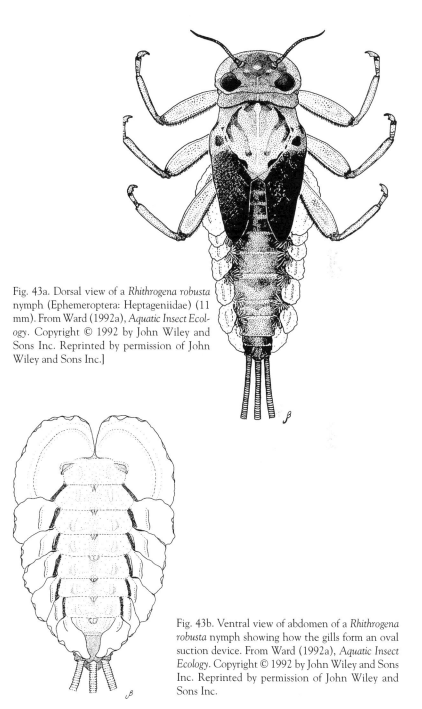

Fig. 43a. Dorsal view of a *Rhithrogena robusta* nymph (Ephemeroptera: Heptageniidae) (11 mm). From Ward (1992a), *Aquatic Insect Ecology*. Copyright © 1992 by John Wiley and Sons Inc. Reprinted by permission of John Wiley and Sons Inc.]

Fig. 43b. Ventral view of abdomen of a *Rhithrogena robusta* nymph showing how the gills form an oval suction device. From Ward (1992a), *Aquatic Insect Ecology*. Copyright © 1992 by John Wiley and Sons Inc. Reprinted by permission of John Wiley and Sons Inc.

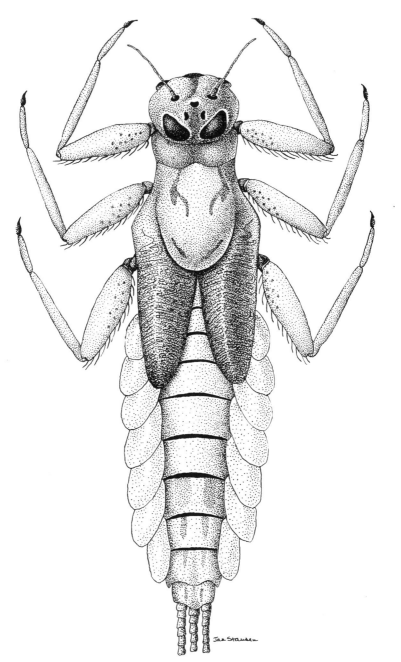

Fig. 44. Dorsal view of a *Cinygmula* sp. nymph (Ephemeroptera: Heptageniidae) (9 mm).

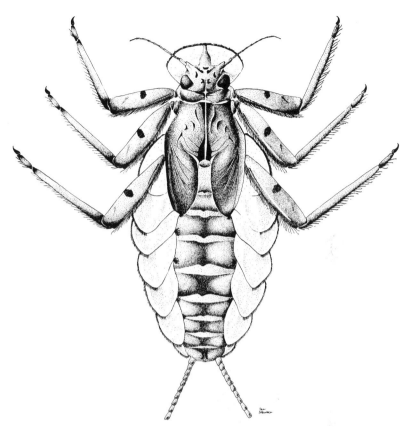

Fig. 45. Dorsal view of an *Epeorus longimanus* nymph (Ephemeroptera: Heptageniidae) (8 mm).

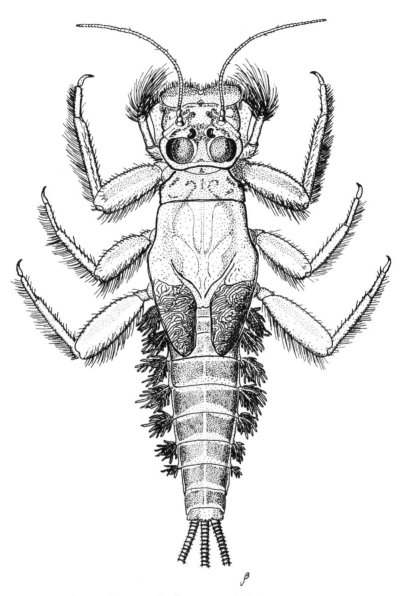

Fig. 46. Dorsal view of a *Traverella albertana* nymph (Ephemeroptera: Leptophlebiidae) (11 mm).

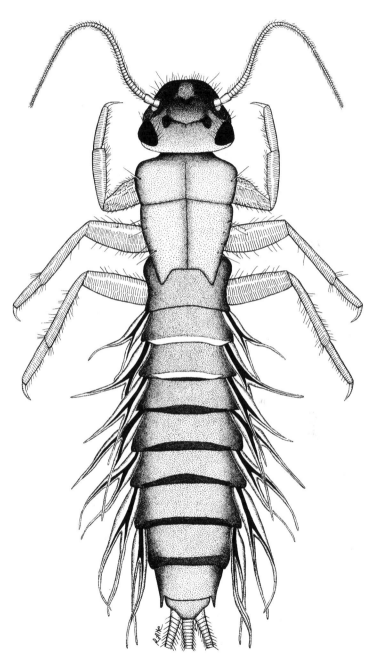

Fig. 47. Dorsal view of a *Paraleptophlebia heteronea* nymph (Ephemeroptera: Leptophlebiidae) (8 mm).

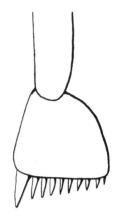

Fig. 48. The spatulate claw *of Camelobaetidius* sp. (Ephemeroptera: Baetidae).

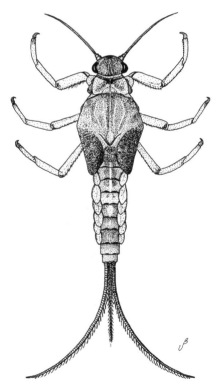

Fig. 49. Dorsal view of a *Baetis tricaudatus* nymph (Ephemeroptera: Baetidae) (8 mm).
From Ward (1992a), *Aquatic Insect Ecology*. Copyright © 1992 by John Wiley and Sons
Inc. Reprinted by permission of John Wiley and Sons Inc.

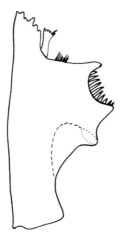

Fig. 50. Left mandible indicating setal tuft of *Fallceon quilleri* (Ephemeroptera: Baetidae).

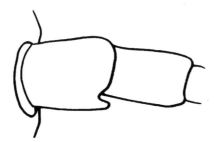

Fig. 51. Antennal scape indicating distal notch of *Pseudocloeon* sp. (Ephemeroptera: Baetidae).

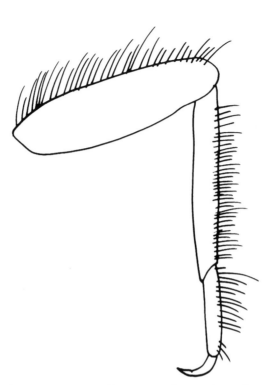

Fig. 52. Right foreleg indicating row of long setae on femora, tibia, and tarsus of *Acentrella* sp. (Ephemeroptera: Baetidae).

Fig. 53. Labial palp indicating thumb of *Baetis* sp. (Ephemeroptera: Baetidae).

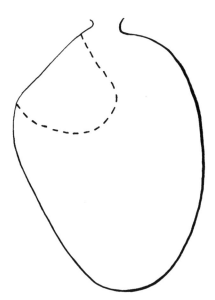

Fig. 54. A gill of *Callibaetis* sp. showing the recurved flap (dashed line) (Ephemeroptera: Baetidae).

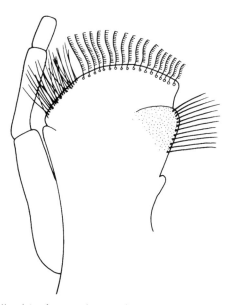

Fig. 55. The maxilla of *Ameletus* sp. showing the pectinate comb of spines (the "diatom rake") (Ephemeroptera: Ameletidae).

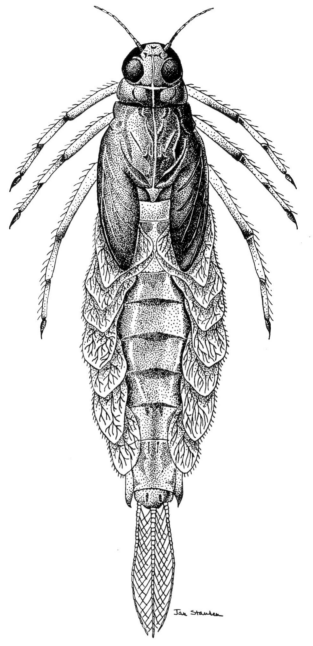

Fig. 56. Dorsal view of a *Siphlonurus occidentalis* nymph (Ephemeroptera: Siphlonuridae) (13 mm).

TRICHOPTERA

Most Trichoptera (caddisflies) are restricted to cool lotic habitats; all North American families have representatives in cool running waters (Wiggins 1996). However, the order is also well represented in warm lotic and lentic waters. Caddisfly larvae collectively occupy a diverse array of habitats and feeding types. Wiggins and Mackay (1978) attribute this high ecological diversity to niche segregation made possible by silk production. For example, different mesh sizes of net-spinning species enable segregation of food resources between closely related forms.

Fourteen of the currently recognized twenty-six North American families of Trichoptera (Wiggins 1996) have been recorded from Colorado mountain streams (Table 9). Molannidae and Phryganeidae are primarily lentic families and have been recorded from Colorado. Herrmann, Ruiter, and Unzicker (1986) and Ruiter (1990, 1999) sumarize distributions for Colorado caddisflies. The higher classification and phylogeny of the Trichoptera are discussed by Frania and Wiggins (1997) and Morse (1997). John C. Morse (Clemson University) provides a searchable world checklist of Trichoptera, including new taxa and taxonomic changes (http://entweb.clemson.edu/database/trichoptindex.htm). See Appendix C for the known Colorado distribution of mountain stream Trichoptera species.

Trichoptera larvae are highly diversified in their feeding mechanisms; each feeding type is well developed in at least a few genera. Several groups are highly specialized filter-feeders that use silk to construct intricate capture nets (Wallace and Merritt 1980).

Case building is a characteristic feature of the order (Wiggins and Wichard 1989; Frania and Wiggins 1997). Even species lacking larval cases construct cases for pupation. Cases may be formed of silk (secreted from labial glands) alone, or various materials (e.g., sand, leaf fragments) may be cemented together to form the case. Cases may be attached to the substrate (fixed) or may be portable.

Most caddisflies have five larval instars. The final larval instar constructs a pupal case (in species without larval cases) or seals itself in the larval case for pupation. The pupal stage (Fig. 57) lasts only two to three weeks in most species. In temperate areas most species are univoltine.

Wiggins (1996) provides excellent generic keys to all North American larvae and much valuable ecological data. Taxonomic keys for specific groups are referred to in the following discussion of individual families.

Table 9—Known representation of caddisflies (Trichoptera) in Colorado mountain streams.

Order Family	Number of Genera		Number of Species	
TRICHOPTERA	56	(148)	125	(1358)
Apataniidae	2	(5)	3	(32)
Beraeidae	0	(1)	0	(3)
Brachycentridae	3	(5)	4	(34)
Calamoceratidae	0	(3)	0	(5)
Dipseudopsidae	0	(1)	0	(5)
Ecnomidae	0	(1)	0	(1)
Glossosomatidae	5	(6)	10	(81)
Goeridae	0	(4)	0	(11)
Helicopsychidae	1	(1)	1	(5)
Hydrobiosidae	0	(1)	0	(3)
Hydropsychidae	5	(11)	11	(146)
Hydroptilidae	8	(16)	18	(226)
Lepidostomatidae	1	(2)	6	(81)
Leptoceridae	3	(8)	8	(113)
Limnephilidae	19	(39)	33	(243)
Molannidae	0	(2)	0	(7)
Odontoceridae	0	(6)	0	(13)
Philopotamidae	3	(3)	3	(42)
Phryganeidae	0	(10)	0	(28)
Polycentropodidae	1	(6)	4	(70)
Psychomyiidae	1	(4)	1	(17)
Rhyacophildae	1	(2)	17	(129)
Rossianidae	0	(2)	0	(2)
Sericostomatidae	0	(3)	0	(14)
Uenoidae	3	(5)	4	(46)
Xiphocentronidae	0	(1)	0	(1)

Source: Numbers in the first and third columns are totals from Herrmann et al. (1986), Ruiter (1990), and Ruiter (1999) and include typical lotic species; numbers in parentheses are totals for North America and include both lotic and lentic species. Totals are derived from Morse (1993) and Wiggins (1996).

Note: See Appendix C for known distributions of Colorado species by major drainage basin.

Several ecological studies deal specifically with Trichoptera of Colorado mountain streams (Dodds and Hisaw 1925b; Mecom 1972a and b; Ward 1981, 1987; Canton and Ward 1981a; Stanford and Ward 1981; DeWalt et al. 1994; Ruse and Herrmann 2000).

Many cased caddis larvae have spacing humps on the first abdominal segment (Fig. 58) to permit circulation of oxygenated water through the case (Williams, Tavares, and Bryant 1987). Current is generated by abdominal undulation. A lateral hair fringe along each side of the abdomen (Fig. 77) aids in creating current. Setal areas are referred to by number in the keys according to Wiggins (1996), as shown in Fig. 70. Caddis larvae have anal prolegs (Fig. 78), the structures of which provide important key characters. The thoracic legs of caddis larvae have the same basic segments (femur, tibia, and so on) as stonefly nymphs (see Fig. 15); however, some of these segments may be subdivided. Most larvae have filamentous gills along the abdomen (Fig. 75). For more details on larval morphology see Wiggins (1996).

KEY TO COLORADO FAMILIES OF LOTIC TRICHOPTERA LARVAE

1. Larva with case of sand grains in shape of snail shell (Fig. 59).......
   ....Helicopsychidae (p. 106)
   Larva without case, or case not in shape of snail shell.................2

2. Dorsum of each thoracic segment covered by sclerotized plates (see Fig. 78)...3
   Metanotum (and sometimes also mesonotum) almost entirely membranous; may have small sclerites but not covered by large sclerotized plates (Figs. 61, 64)..4

3. Mature larva usually <6 mm long; abdomen without lateral gills; purse-shaped case; enlarged abdomen (Fig. 63)............Hydroptilidae (p. 107)
   Mature larva larger; abdomen with conspicuous gills; without case, in fixed retreat adjacent to feeding net; abdomen similar to thorax in thickness (Fig. 78)................................Hydropsychidae (p. 108)

4. Antennae at least six times as long as wide, arising near base of mandibles; tubular portable case.....................Leptoceridae (p. 109)
   Antennae very short and inconspicuous, at most three times as long as wide...5

5. Mesonotum without large sclerotized plates (small sclerites may be present)..6
   Mesonotum almost completely covered by sclerotized plates..........10

6. Last abdominal segment with a dorsal sclerotized plate (Fig. 64)
  7
   Last abdominal segment without a dorsal sclerotized plate 8

7. Portable case in shape of tortoiseshell (Fig. 64); basally, anal prolegs broadly attached to ninth abdominal segment.................
   ....Glossosomatidae (p. 109)

Larvae without case or fixed retreat; most of anal proleg free of ninth abdominal segment (Fig. 69)..............Rhyacophilidae (p. 110)

8. Labrum membranous and T-shaped (may be retracted in preserved larvae) (see Fig. 80); larva in finger-shaped net attached to undersides of rocks..Philopotamidae (p. 110)

   Labrum sclerotized, not T-shaped..9

9. Trochantin of prothoracic leg with pointed tip (Fig. 82); retreat a fixed trumpet-shaped silk net, or fixed tubes with flared ends.......
   ....Polycentropodidae (p. 110)

   Trochantin of prothoracic leg broad and hatchet-shaped (Fig. 83); retreat tubular and sometimes branched, attached to rocks or logs..Psychomyiidae (p. 111)

10. First abdominal segment with lateral and usually dorsal spacing humps (Figs. 58, 73)..11

    First abdominal segment without dorsal or lateral spacing humps (Fig. 61)....................................Brachycentridae (p. 111)

11. First abdominal segment with lateral, but not dorsal, spacing humps (Fig. 60); antennae very close to anterior margin of eye...............
    ....Lepidostomatidae (p. 112)

    First abdominal segment with both dorsal and lateral spacing humps; antennae at least as close to margin of head capsule as to eye.........
   12

12. Mesonotal plates with distinct anteromedian emargination or notch
    ....Uenoidae (p. 112)

    Mesonotal plates lacking distinct anteromedian emargination or notch..13

13. Mandibles toothed (Fig. 71); case composed of variable materials; common....................................Limnephilidae (p. 112)

    Mandibles with scraper blades (Fig. 72); case of mineral materials; uncommon....................................Apataniidae (p. 114)

Family Helicopsychidae. This family is represented in Colorado by only one confirmed species, *Helicopsyche borealis.* The case of sand grains resembles a coiled snail shell (Fig. 59). Larvae are tolerant of high temperatures and have been collected in Yellowstone National Park from a spring that reaches 34°C (Wiggins 1996). Specimens were collected from a warm spring (25°C) at an elevation of 3,109 m near Fairplay, Colorado (Ward, unpublished data), but they are normally restricted to low-elevation streams (Ward 1981). *Helicopsyche borealis* larvae feed primarily on detritus (Mecom 1972b).

Family Hydroptilidae. These are known as the "microcaddis" because of their small size (mature larvae are less than 6 mm long). Last instar larvae of the eight genera reported from Colorado mountain streams may be separated as follows:

1. Pronotum, mesonotum, and metanotum each with sclerotized plates divided into two halves by a midline suture; portable cases...........2

    Midline suture present only on pronotum (Fig. 62), absent from mesonotum and metanotum; flattened, elliptical silken retreats attached to rocks ....*Leucotrichia*

2. Hind tarsi usually short and thick, similar to tarsal claw in length (Fig. 63) or shorter; or if hind tarsi are slender and longer than claws, there is a prominent lobe extending from protibia; anal prolegs appressed to body, only claws projecting beyond body outline.......3

    Hind tarsi twice as long as tarsal claw or longer; anal prolegs projecting beyond body...7

3. Tarsal claws thick and abruptly curved, each with a thick, blunt spur at base; case of two symmetrical valves of silk............*Stactobiella*

    Tarsal claws slender and smoothly curved (Fig. 63), each with a thin, pointed spur at base...4

4. Middle and hind legs about 2.5 times length of forelegs; case entirely of silk, shaped like a flask in lateral view.................*Oxyethira*

    Middle and hind legs a maximum of 1.5 times length of forelegs (Fig. 63)..5

5. Three long gill filaments arising from end of abdomen (two gills visible in Fig. 63); case of two laterally compressed valves covered with sand grains (Fig. 63)...................................*Hydroptila*

    Posterior of abdomen without gills...6

6. Small dark central sclerites on dorsum of each abdominal segment; case usually similar to *Hydroptila* (Fig. 63).................*Ochrotrichia*

    Dark central sclerites absent from dorsum of all or most abdominal segments; case of two laterally compressed valves of algal filaments arranged in a concentric pattern.................................*Agraylea*

7. Well-developed lateral hair fringe along abdomen; case cylindrical, composed of sand grains..*Neotrichia*

   Lateral hair fringe lacking; case cylindrical, of silk without attached sand grains; large rivers..*Mayatrichia*

There are no satisfactory species keys for larval hydroptilids. These are the smallest caddisflies occurring in Colorado. Mature *Neotrichia* larvae are only 2 mm long. The first four larval instars do not construct cases. Only the final larval instar and pupae reside in a case. Little is known of the biology or ecology of hydroptilids. Larvae of most species are thought to feed primarily on algae.

Family Hydropsychidae. Larvae of the three common genera of hydropsychids in Colorado mountain streams are separated as follows:

1. Stridulator (spur) at base of front legs pointed (Fig. 78), not forked (stridulator may be concealed in preserved specimens; if so, gently pull legs away from body)..*Arctopsyche*

   Stridulator forked..2

2. A pair of enlarged sclerites in intersegmental fold posterior to prosternal plate (Fig. 79) (it may be necessary to stretch specimen to expose the intersegmental fold)..*Hydropsyche*

   Sclerites absent or only tiny sclerites present in intersegmental fold posterior to prosternal plate..*Cheumatopsyche*

The three most common species of *Hydropsyche* (*H. cockerelli, H. occidentalis,* and *H. oslari*) in Colorado mountain streams can usually be separated by markings on the larval head capsule (see Alstad 1980), but the work of Schefter and Wiggins (1986) needs to be consulted for positive identification of *H. cockerelli, H. oslari,* and other *morosa* group species occurring in Colorado. There are no suitable species keys for larval *Cheumatopsyche*. Givens and Smith (1980) provide larval keys to species of western *Arctopsyche* and *Parapsyche*. Currently, only *A. grandis* has been reported from Colorado mountain streams, but some authorities recognize a second species, *A. inermis*. Morse (1993) and Morse and Holzental (1996) rank *Arctopsyche* and *Parapsyche* as belonging to a separate family, the Arctopsychidae. Similarly, some authories recognize the genus *Ceratopsyche* for the *Hydropsyche morosa* species group (see Schefter and Wiggins 1986 for explanation). We follow Wiggins's (1996) classification of this family.

Hydropsychid larvae spin feeding nets on the surface of rocks, logs, and other structures (e.g., bridge abutments) in the water. They reside in a rough shelter attached to the net from which they venture forth to feed on materials adhering to the mesh. Mesh size varies according to species, and there is a progressive increase in aperture size from early to late instars of the same species (Wallace and Merritt 1980). Hydropsychid larvae may constitute a major portion of the total benthic fauna in habitats, such as lake outlets, that contain high concentrations of organic seston (Ward and Short 1978).

Family Leptoceridae. Larvae of the two common genera of leptocerids occurring in Colorado mountain streams are distinguished as follows:

1. Maxillary palps extending far beyond anterior edge of labrum; case cylindrical, composed of various materials............................*Oecetis*

   Maxillary palps extending little, if any, beyond anterior edge of labrum; case an extremely long, tapered cylinder.............*Nectopsyche*

Haddock (1977) provides larval keys to North American species of *Nectopsyche,* and Floyd (1995) published a key to *Oecetis* larvae. Species of *Nectopsyche* are warm-adapted and normally occur only in slow-flowing lower reaches of mountain streams. They are often associated with beds of aquatic plants. Larvae tend to be omnivorous. Species of *Oecetis* are usually found in cooler water than are *Nectopsyche.* The larvae are predators. Occasionally, larvae of *Ceraclea* can be collected from Colorado lotic systems. Larvae are easily recognized by a pair of dark curved bars on the mesonotum.

Family Glossosomatidae. The five genera of glossosomatids occurring in Colorado mountain streams may be distinguished as follows:

1. Mesonotum without sclerites (Fig. 64).......................................2

   Mesonotum with two or three sclerites....................................3

2. Lateral view of pronotum (leg removed) as in Fig. 65......*Glossosoma*

   Lateral view of pronotum (leg removed) as in Fig. 66.........*Anagapetus*

3. Mesonotum with three sclerites 4

   Mesonotum with two sclerites ....*Agapetus*

4. Tarsal claw with slender seta arising from concave surface (Fig. 68).....
   ....*Protoptila*

Tarsal claw with stout seta arising from concave surface (Fig. 67).....
....*Culoptila*

There are no satisfactory species keys to western North American glossosomatid larvae. The larvae in this family construct tortoiseshell or saddle cases (Fig. 64), which enable them to feed while completely beneath the case. They reside primarily on the upper surfaces of rocks submerged in the current and feed by grazing on periphyton and entrapped fine detritus.

Family Rhyacophilidae. Rhyacophila (Fig. 69) is the largest caddisfly genus, and is the only genus of this family in Colorado. Smith (1968), Wold (1973), and Peck and Smith (1978) provide species keys to larvae. Larval *Rhyacophila* are free-living (caseless). They are important components of Colorado mountain streams, especially at high and middle elevations. As many as seven species of *Rhyacophila* have been collected from the same riffle (Ward 1981). The majority of species are predators, but some feed on vascular plant tissue and algae (Thut 1969).

Family Philopotamidae. Larvae of the three genera from this family known to occur in Colorado mountain streams are separated as follows:

1. Anterior margin of frontoclypeus with a prominent notch (Fig. 80)..*Chimarra*

   Anterior margin of frontoclypeus without a prominent notch.........2

2. Stridulator (trochantin) at base of front legs projecting freely to form an elongate, fingerlike process (Fig. 81).................*Dolophilodes*

   Stridulator (trochantin) at base of front legs projects only a short distance and does not form an elongate, fingerlike process...........
   ....*Wormaldia*

Each of these genera has but a single species occurring in Colorado mountain streams (*C. utahensis, D. aequalis,* and *W. gabriella*).

Philopotamid larvae spin elongate, saclike nets, of which the open (upstream) ends are usually attached to the undersides of rocks. Larvae live within the nets, where they move about eating the fine particles from the inner net surface.

Family Polycentropodidae. Several species of *Polycentropus* have been reported from Colorado mountain streams. Larvae reside within fixed silken retreats that function to capture the small aquatic animals upon which they feed.

Family Psychomyiidae. Psychomyia flavida is the only species from this family known to occur in Colorado mountain streams. Larvae reside in meandering, sometimes branched, silken tubes attached to the surfaces of rocks and submerged logs. Larvae are omnivorous, feeding on algae and some detritus and animals.

Family Brachycentridae. Larvae are unique among all portable case makers in lacking both dorsal and lateral humps on the first abdominal segment. Four-sided cases are very characteristic of *Brachycentrus americanus.* Larvae of the three genera may be separated as follows:

1. Middle and hind legs with tibia produced to form a prominent distal process from which spines arise (Fig. 61); middle and hind legs long; case either distinctly four-sided or slightly rounded and composed of plant fragments arranged transversely and/or fine-grained minerals (Fig. 61)..*Brachycentrus*

   Tibia of middle and hind legs without prominent distal process; middle and hind legs shorter; case usually round in cross section 2

2. Transverse ridge of pronotum not extending to anterior edge..... ....*Amiocentrus*

   Transverse ridge of pronotum extends to anterior edge.............. ....*Micrasema*

Brachycentrus is the only common genus of this family in Colorado, and larvae use silk to temporarily attach the ventral lip of their cases to the substrate when feeding. The legs are held in the current and food particles are filtered from the water column. Larvae also feed by grazing on the substrate. A variety of materials are ingested, including various algae, detritus, and small insects. *Brachycentrus occidentalis* is often exceedingly abundant in some of the larger streams, such as the Colorado River above and below Glenwood Springs and the Arkansas River at Salida/Texas Creek (locally referred to as the Mother's Day caddisfly hatch on the Arkansas River). Flint's (1984) revision allows separation of adult males and larvae of the two Colorado species (*B. americanus* and *B. occidentalis*). There is only one species each of *Amiocentrus* (*A. aspilus*) and *Micrasema* (*M. bactro*) recorded from Colorado.

Family Lepidostomatidae. Only one genus, *Lepidostoma*, from this family occurs in Colorado. *Lepidostoma* is often abundant in Colorado mountain streams and springs (Appendix C), but satisfactory species keys are unavailable for larvae (Weaver 1988). The larvae construct portable cases of sand grains (Fig. 60) or plant fragments. Larvae are detritivore shredders.

Family Uenoidae. The genus *Neothremma*, traditionally placed in the Limnephilidae, was transferred to the family Uenoidae by Wiggins, Weaver, and Unzicker (1985). Vineyard and Wiggins (1988) added the genera *Neophylax and Oligophlebodes* to this family. These three genera can be separated as follows:

1. Pronotum with prominent longitudinal ridges (Fig. 76)...............
    ....*Oligophlebodes*

    Pronotum without prominent longitudinal ridges.......................2

2. Larvae and case extremely slender; abdominal gills lacking (Fig. 77)
    ....*Neothremma*

    Larvae and case not slender, case of coarse rock fragments, larger fragments along each side; abdominal gills present...........*Neophylax*

Presently, there are no suitable species keys to the larvae of *Oligophlebodes*. Both *Neothremma* and *Neophylax* are represented in small mountain streams and springs of Colorado by single species (*Neothremma alicia* and *Neophylax splendens*). Larvae are grazer-scrapers feeding on diatomaceous film and fine particulate organic matter on rocky substrates.

Family Limnephilidae. The fifteen genera of limnephilids reported from Colorado mountain streams may be separated as follows:

1. Most abdominal gills single..2

    Most abdominal gills of dorsal and ventral rows branched, although lateral gills may be single..6

2. Metanotal sa 1 and sa 2 sclerites large; distance between sa 2 sclerites not greater than two times the maximum dimension of one sa 2 sclerite; larva and case relatively long and slender........*Ecclisomyia*

    Metanotal sa 1 and sa 2 sclerites smaller; distance between sa 2 sclerites more than twice the maximum dimension of one sa 2 sclerite....3

3. Large single sclerite at base of lateral spacing humps enclosing posterior half of hump; case a flattened tube of leaves or bark......*Chyranda*

One or two small sclerites at base of lateral spacing hump.............4

4. Two sclerites at base of lateral spacing hump (Fig. 73); case a straight tube of rock and wood fragments.............................*Psychoglypha*

    One elongate sclerite at posterior edge of base of lateral spacing hump...5

5. Sclerite at base of lateral spacing hump short, its longest dimension equal to about one-half basal width of hump; case of irregularly arranged pieces of bark, usually a smooth cylinder, sometimes three-sided..*Homophylax*

    Sclerite at base of lateral spacing hump elongate, its longest dimension equivalent to basal width of hump; case of twigs or gravel, or of leaves...*Pycnopsyche*

6. Most gills with three branches, none with more than four (Fig. 74)..7

    Some gills with more than four branches.............................14

7. Femur of hind leg with two long setae on ventral edge.................10

    Femur of hind leg with more than two long setae on ventral edge 8

8. Metanotal sa 1 sclerites fused along mid-dorsal line into a single sclerite; case a hollowed twig or composed of wood fragments.... ....*Amphicosmoecus*

    Metanotal sa 1 sclerites clearly separated; case of rock fragments.....9

9. Tibiae with several pairs of stout spurs (Fig. 74).............*Dicosmoecus*

    Tibiae with one pair of stout spurs...........................*Onocosmoecus*

10. Dorsal chloride epithelia present on abdomen.............................11

    Dorsal chloride epithelia absent on abdomen.............................12

11. Pronotum with short, stout spines at anterolateral corner.............. ....*Asynarchus*

    Pronotum without short, stout spines at anterolateral corner........... ....*Anabolia*

12. Lateral sclerite of anal proleg with short, stout spines.................13

    Lateral sclerite of anal proleg without short, stout spines................ ....*Limnephilus*

13. Dark bands on tibiae and tarsi of all legs; case of twigs and bark.......
....*Glyphopsyche*
    Legs without dark bands...*Clistoronia*

14. Gill row along lateral hair fringe single and restricted to abdominal segment 2, and sometimes 3; case of rock fragments; uncommon....
....*Psychoronia*
    Gill row along lateral hair fringe present on abdominal segments 2–4 or 2–5, and at least some with more than one branch; case of rock fragments or plant fragments (Fig. 75); common...........*Hesperophylax*

There are no suitable species keys available for all limnephilid larvae. Six genera are each represented by a single species in Colorado (*Amphicosmoecus canax, Chyranda centralis, Glyphopsyche irrorata, Homophylax flavipennis, Onocosmoecus unicolor,* and *Psychoronia costalis*). Parker and Wiggins (1985) provide a key to the larvae of the common genus, *Hesperophylax*. Ruiter (1995) recently reviewed the adults of the genus *Limnephilus*, recording numerous species from Colorado. *Limnephilus lithus* is one of the few species in Colorado found primarily in lotic habitats, usually of lower elevations. Ruiter (2000) provides a key to the genera of the adults of the Limnephilidae and relatives.

Members of this large family are well represented in a wide variety of aquatic environments in Colorado and occur in all major habitat types. Most larvae are either shredders or scrapers. All larvae bear portable cases. The type of case is highly variable; however, species of mountain streams tend to construct cases primarily of rock fragments, whereas plant fragments are more commonly used in lentic habitats.

Family Apataniidae. Gall and Wiggins (in Wiggins 1996) placed four limnephilid genera in the Apataniidae. Two genera, *Allomyia* (formerly *Imania*) and sometimes *Apatania*, occur in small mountain streams.

1. Metanotal sa 1 sclerite present, well defined, about the size of sa 2; top of head flattened (Fig. 58)...*Allomyia*
    Metanotal sa 1 absent; top of head smoothly curved.............*Apatania*

Hermann, Ruiter, and Unzicker (1986) list two species of *Allomyia* that are usually restricted to high-elevation streams above 2,700 m. *Apatania zonella* is usually associated with high-elevation lakes, but adults have been collected near streams.

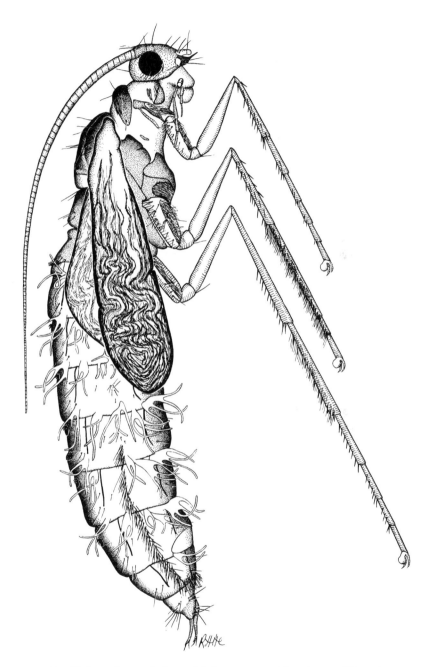

Fig. 57. Lateral view of a limnephilid pupa removed from its case (22 mm).

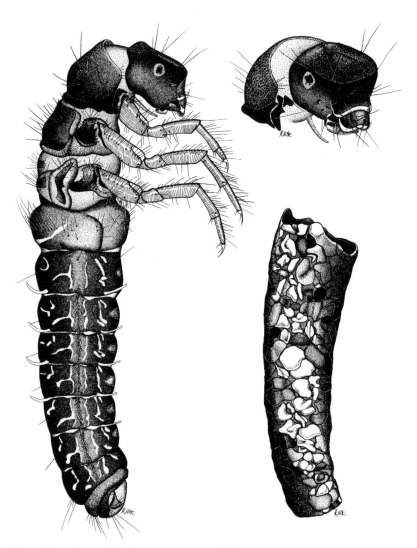

Fig. 58. Lateral view of an *Allomyia tripunctata* (?) larva (6 mm), case, and larval head (all in different scales). Note dorsal and lateral spacing humps on first abdominal segments (Trichoptera: Apataniidae).

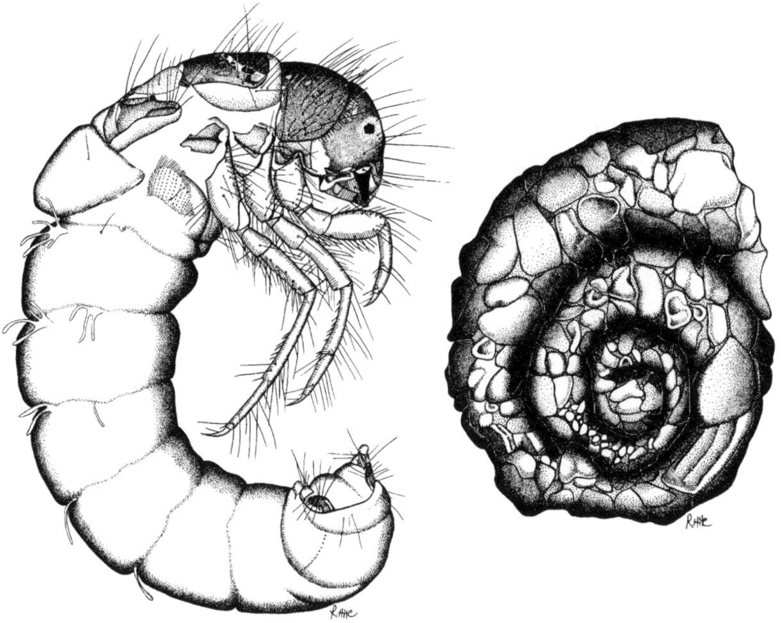

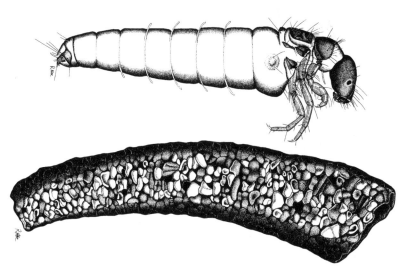

Fig. 59. Lateral view of a *Helicopsyche borealis* larva (4 mm) and case (different scales) (Trichoptera: Helicopsychidae).

Fig. 60. Lateral view of a *Lepidostoma ormeum* larva (5 mm) and case (Trichoptera: Lepidostomatidae).

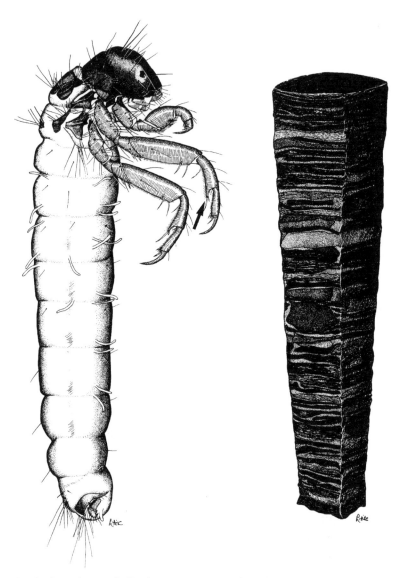

Fig. 61. Lateral view of a *Brachycentrus americanus* larva (9 mm) and case (Trichoptera: Brachycentridae) (arrow indicates distal process of tibia).

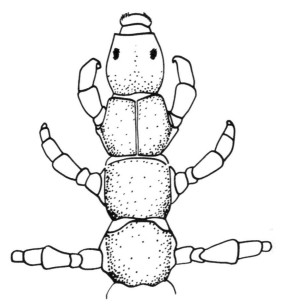

Fig. 62. Dorsal view of *Leucotrichia pictipes* larva (Trichoptera: Hydroptilidae).

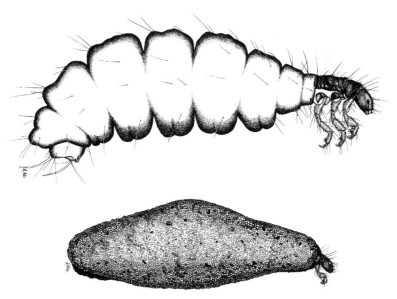

Fig. 63. Lateral view of a *Hydroptila* sp. larva (3 mm) and case (different scales) (Trichoptera: Hydroptilidae).

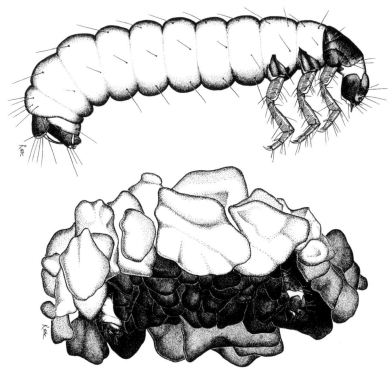

Fig. 64. Lateral view of a *Glossosoma ventrale* larva (5 mm) and case (different scales) (Trichoptera: Glossosomatidae).

Fig. 65. Lateral view of pronotum of *Glossosoma* with leg removed (arrow indicates one-third excised anterolateral portion of pronotum).

Fig. 66. Lateral view of pronotum of *Anagapetus* with leg removed (arrow indicates two-thirds excised anterolateral portion of pronotum).

Fig. 67. Tarsal claw of *Culoptila*.

Fig. 68. Tarsal claw of *Protoptila*.

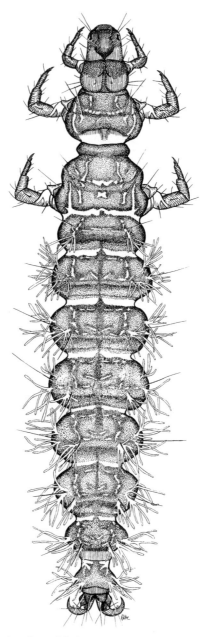

Fig. 69. Dorsal view of a *Rhyacophila brunnea* larva (Trichoptera: Rhyacophilidae) (12 mm). From Ward (1992a), *Aquatic Insect Ecology*. Copyright © 1992 by John Wiley and Sons Inc. Reprinted by permission of John Wiley and Sons Inc.

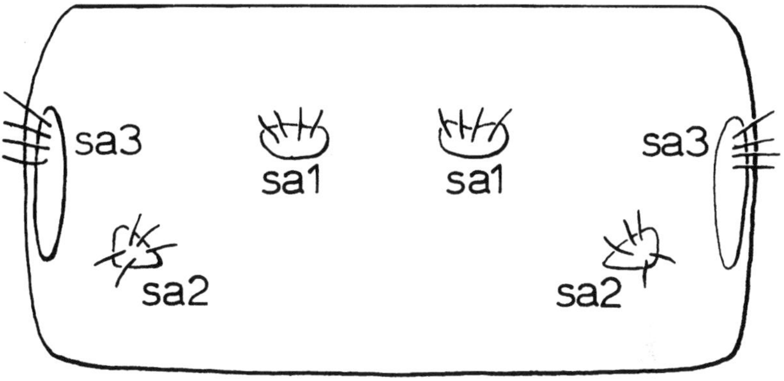

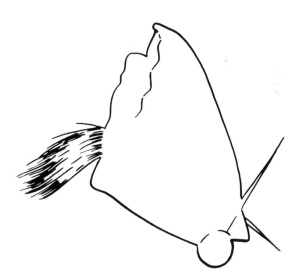

Fig. 70. Dorsal view of the metanotum of a larval caddisfly showing the setal areas.

Fig. 71. Larval mandible indicating toothed lateral surface (Trichoptera: Limnephilidae).

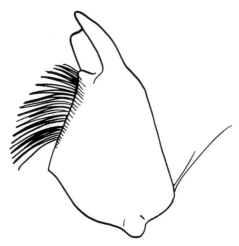

Fig. 72. Larval mandible indicating uniform scraper blades (Trichoptera: Apataniidae).

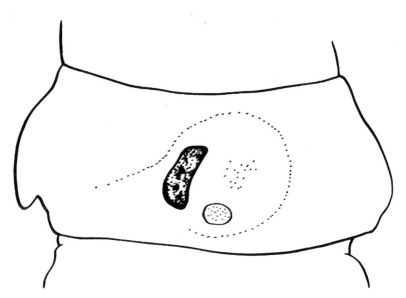

Fig. 73. Larval abdominal segment 1 enlarged, lateral, of *Psychoglypha subborealis* (Trichoptera: Limnephilidae).

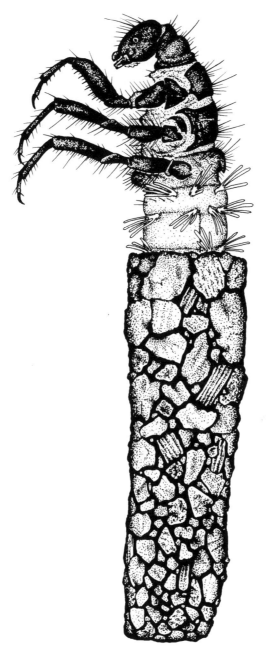

Fig. 74. Lateral view of a *Dicosmoecus atripes* larva (19 mm) and case (Trichoptera: Limnephilidae).

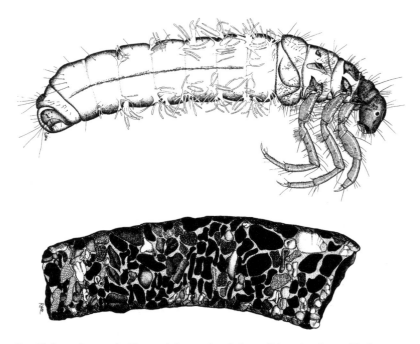

Fig. 75. Lateral view of a *Hesperophylax occidentalis* larva (16 mm) and case (Trichoptera: Limnephilidae).

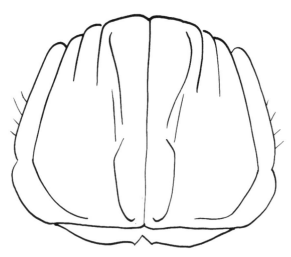

Fig. 76. Dorsal view of larval thorax *Oligophlebodes* sp. (Trichoptera: Uenoidae).

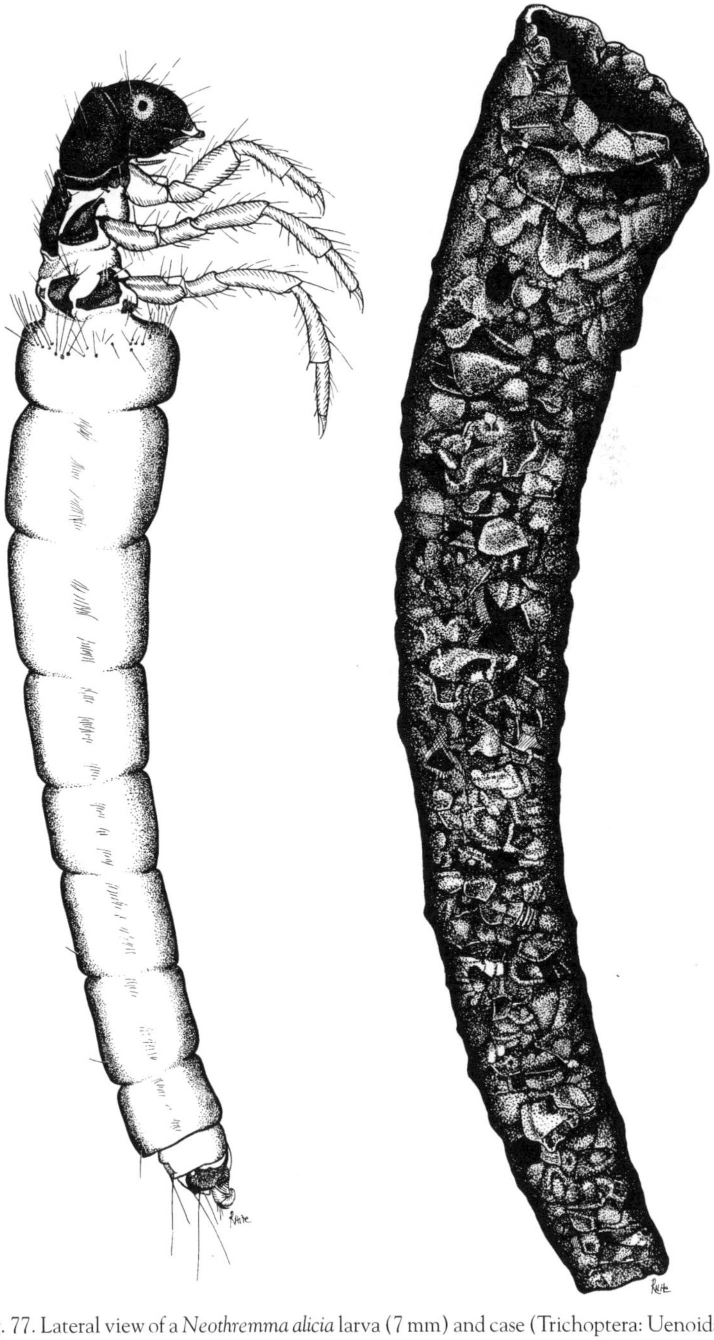

Fig. 77. Lateral view of a *Neothremma alicia* larva (7 mm) and case (Trichoptera: Uenoidae).

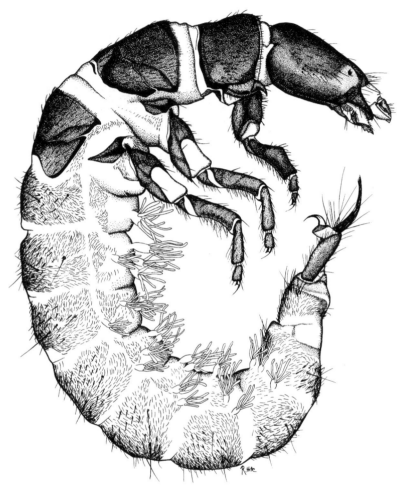

Fig. 78. Lateral view of an *Arctopsyche grandis* larva (Trichoptera: Hydropsychidae) (26 mm).

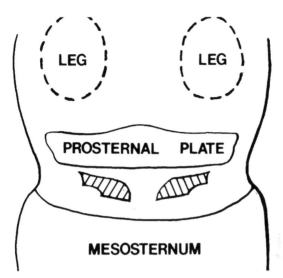

Fig. 79. Sclerites (crosshatched) of intersegmental fold posterior to prosternal plate of *Hydropsyche*. Points of attachment of front legs are indicated.

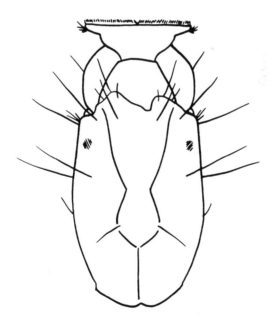

Fig. 80. Dorsal view of head of *Chimarra* sp. (Trichoptera: Philopotamidae).

Fig. 81. Lateral view of fore trochantin of *Dolophilodes* sp. (Trichoptera: Philopotamidae).

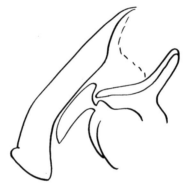

Fig. 82. Lateral view of prothorax of *Polycentropus* sp. (Trichoptera: Polycentropodidae).

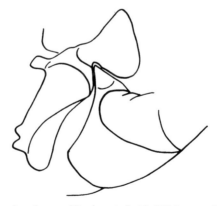

Fig. 83. Lateral view of prothorax of *Psychomyia flavida* (Trichoptera: Polycentropodidae).

COLEOPTERA

The Coleoptera (beetles) have more species than all other insects combined. The vast majority, however, are terrestrial. Most species that are aquatic inhabit lentic, rather than lotic, habitats. Both adults and larvae of most aquatic beetles reside underwater, although adults may leave the water for dispersal flights. Typically, last instar larvae move onto land to pupate, and the adults that emerge from the pupal chambers return to the water. Larvae of some aquatic beetles have gills or obtain sufficient oxygen through the general body surface, but others must periodically travel to the surface to obtain atmospheric air. Larvae of a few groups tap the air spaces of underwater plants. Adults of many aquatic beetles carry an air bubble that must be periodically replenished at the surface. Only certain groups that are highly adapted to life in cold, well-oxygenated running waters have become independent of atmospheric air. Most aquatic beetles have three to eight larval instars. Nearly all aquatic species of the Temperate Zone are univoltine. The name Coleoptera ("sheath-winged") refers to the hardened first pair of wings, the elytra (plural of elytron), which cover the membranous second pair of wings of adult beetles (Fig. 84). The elytra are held forward during flight, which is performed by the second pair of wings. Other morphological structures of adult beetles are illustrated in Figs. 84 and 85. Larval structures are shown in Fig. 86. Brown's (1976) guide to the aquatic dryopoid beetles of the United States includes the families most highly adapted to running waters (Elmidae, Psephenidae, Dryopidae). The guide contains species keys to adults and generic keys to larvae as well as ecological and distributional data. Crowson's (1981) *Biology of the Coleoptera* and Arnett and Thomas (2001) cover the taxonomy and biology of the aquatic beetle families. Remarkably little work has been directed toward aquatic beetles of Colorado. Given the limited data available, it would be meaningless to present the known distribution of aquatic beetles, as has been done for stoneflies, mayflies, and caddisflies (Appendices A, B, and C). The following keys to families of adult and larval beetles include the groups most commonly collected in running-water habitats in mountainous regions of Colorado. However, with the exception of three families, these beetles are only rarely collected in high-gradient mountain streams. They occur in slower reaches of running waters as well as in lentic habitats, or they inhabit special lotic environments such as spring brooks and intermittent streams. Several

genera of Elmidae, and *Helichus* of the Dryopidae, are especially characteristic of rocky streams (as are the Psephenidae or "water pennies,"
which apparently do not occur in Colorado). Elmid beetles are often
the only coleopterans in benthic samples collected from Colorado mountain streams, and this is the only family for which generic keys are
included herein.

KEY TO COLORADO FAMILIES OF ADULT COLEOPTERA

1. Each eye divided by lateral margin of head to appear as separate
    dorsal and ventral eyes...Gyrinidae

    Eyes not divided...2

2. Hind coxae greatly enlarged, forming plates covering much of ab-
    domen and bases of hind legs...Haliplidae

    Hind coxae normal...3

3. Hind coxae with median portion extending posteriorly, thus divid-
    ing first visible abdominal sternite (Fig. 85)...................................4

    Hind coxae not extending posteriorly; first visible abdominal ster-
    nite not divided into two parts by coxae......................................5

4. Hind tarsi and usually tibiae flattened and streamlined, with long,
    stiff swimming hairs (Fig. 85)...Dytiscidae

    Hind tarsi and tibiae cylindrical or subcylindrical and without long,
    stiff swimming hairs.....................Amphizoidae (*Amphizoa lecontei*)

5. Antennae filiform (Fig. 85).....................Elmidae (in part) (p. 133)

    Antennae not filiform; at least some segments enlarged (antennae
    may be concealed beneath head, as in Fig. 87)..............................6

6. Prosternum with a posterior process that fits into a groove on me-
    sosternum (Fig. 85)..8

    Prosternum without such a process..7

7. Antennal club of five segments..............................Hydraenidae

    Antennal club of fewer than five segments (Fig. 87).....Hydrophilidae

8. Antennae very short and thick (usually concealed beneath head),
    with enlarged basal segment and pectinate apical portion.............
    ....Dryopidae (*Helichus*) (p. 135)

    Antennae clubbed (terminal segments, but not basal segments
    enlarged)...Elmidae (in part) (p. 133)

KEY TO COLORADO FAMILIES OF LARVAL COLEOPTERA

1. Legs with five segments; tarsi usually with two claws (Fig. 86).......2

   Legs with three to four segments; tarsi usually with one claw............5

2. Last segment of abdomen with four hooks......................Gyrinidae

   Last abdominal segment without four hooks............................3

3. Abdomen with nine or ten segments; tarsi with single claw.........
   ....Haliplidae

   Abdomen with eight segments; tarsi with two claws....................4

4. Thorax and abdomen flattened; sides of abdomen projecting laterally as thin plates..........................Amphizoidae (*Amphizoa lecontei*)

   Body cylindrical or subcylindrical in cross section; sides of abdomen not projecting laterally as thin plates (Fig. 86)........Dytiscidae

5. Labrum separated from head by a distinct suture; lidlike operculum
   on ventral portion of ninth abdominal segment......Elmidae (p. 133)

   Labrum not represented as a distinct sclerite; operculum lacking on
   ventral portion of ninth abdominal segment............Hydrophilidae

Family Elmidae. Larvae of the four common genera of elmid beetles
inhabiting Colorado mountain streams may be distinguished as follows:

1. Abdomen with pleura (rectangular sclerites along sides of abdomen) on first six or seven segments (Fig. 88)............................2

   Abdomen with pleura on first eight segments; head tuberculate,
   with suberect spines; body subcylindrical, yellowish; mature larvae
   usually >8 mm..*Narpus*

2. Mesopleuron (pleuron of mesothorax) composed of two sclerites
   (Fig. 88)..3

   Mesopleuron composed of one sclerite............................*Optioservus*

3. Body hemicylindrical in cross section................................*Zaitzevia*

   Body subtriangular in cross section............................*Heterlimnius*

Adults of the four common genera of elmid beetles inhabiting Colorado mountain streams may be distinguished as follows:

1. Antennae with eight segments, the apical segment enlarged (more
   enlarged than in Fig. 89); pronotum dark brown with three longitudinal grooves, the median groove longer than the lateral grooves;
   elytra reddish brown, with three ridges near lateral margin; 2–2.5

mm long...*Zaitzevia*

Antennae with ten or eleven segments.................................2

2. Posteriolateral margin of fourth abdominal sternite produced as a tooth, which is bent upward...3

    Posteriolateral margins of abdominal sternites not produced as an upturned tooth; elytra reddish brown with a broad black band across middle...*Narpus*

3. Antennae with ten segments, with last three segments somewhat enlarged; tarsal claws relatively slender; pronotum black; elytra black or dark brown, sometimes reddish at base and in a faint apical spot (Fig. 89)..*Heterlimnius*

    Antennae with eleven segments, the last three segments less enlarged; tarsal claws somewhat larger and more curved........*Optioservus*

Three of the four common genera of elmid beetles are apparently each represented by a single species in Colorado mountain streams (*Narpus concolor*, *Zaitzevia parvula*, and *Heterlimnius corpulentus*). *Optioservus* adults may be keyed to species using White (1978). Brown and White (1978) provide especially useful information on distinguishing various elmid beetles. *Cleptelmis ornata* has also been reported from several Colorado mountain streams. Recently, the widespread genus *Stenelmis* was recorded from the Colorado River near Grand Junction (Schmude and Brown 1991), and is also known from the Green and Yampa Rivers in Dinosaur National Monument. Two additional genera can be collected from large Western Slope rivers of the Colorado River drainage, the widespread *Microcylloepus* (*M. pusillus*) and *Dubiraphia*. *Dubiraphia* has also been collected from small Front Range streams. The biology of the Elmidae is treated by Brown (1987). The Elmidae (riffle beetles) are small, nonswimming beetles of which the vast majority are especially adapted to life in running waters. In high-gradient Colorado streams, elmids are often the only coleopterans encountered; at high elevations *Heterlimnius corpulentus* is often the only beetle collected (Ward 1986). Little ecological work has been conducted on elmid beetles in North America. Three years or more were required to complete the life cycles of five species studied by LeSage and Harper (1976), who reported that the diets consisted of fine detritus and diatoms. Seagle (1982) also found detritus and algae to be the major dietary components of elmid beetles. The genus *Lara* feeds on wood (Anderson et al. 1978).

Family Dryopidae. *Helichus striatus* is the only member of this family occurring in Colorado mountain streams. Only the adults are aquatic. They resemble elmids but are somewhat larger.

Other Families. The remaining families of aquatic beetles occurring in Colorado primarily comprise species inhabiting standing waters or slow-running waters. It is presumed that most species are lentic forms also able to colonize the slower reaches of streams and rivers. Dytiscid (especially the genera *Agabus, Oreodytes, Stictotarsus*) and hydrophilid (especially the genus *Tropisternus*) beetles and members of a few other families are frequently encountered lotic habitats such as spring brooks and intermittent streams. The recent review of the North American dytiscid adults and larvae by Larson, Alarie, and Roughley (2000) provides useful keys and diagnoses for all species. Additionally, the reader is referred to Archangelsky (1997) for a synopsis of the immature stages of the hydrophilids and related families. The coleopteran fauna of such habitats has not been studied sufficiently in Colorado to determine whether the species residing there are in any way adapted to the special conditions.

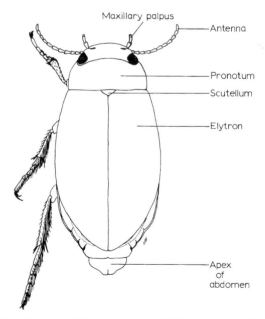

Fig. 84. Dorsal view of adult *Agabus seriatus* (Coleoptera: Dytiscidae) (11 mm).

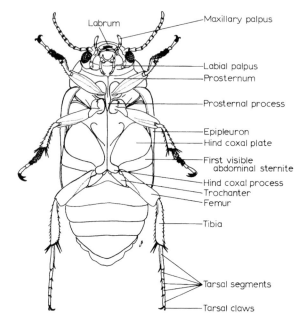

Fig. 85. Ventral view of adult *Agabus seriatus* (Coleoptera: Dytiscidae) (11 mm).

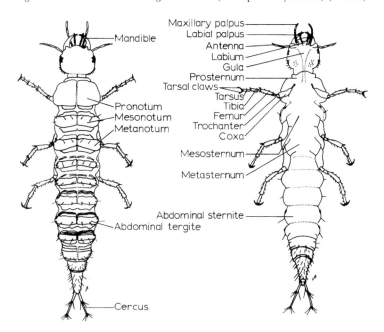

Fig. 86. Dorsal and ventral views of *Agabus* larva (Coleoptera: Dytiscidae) (12 mm).

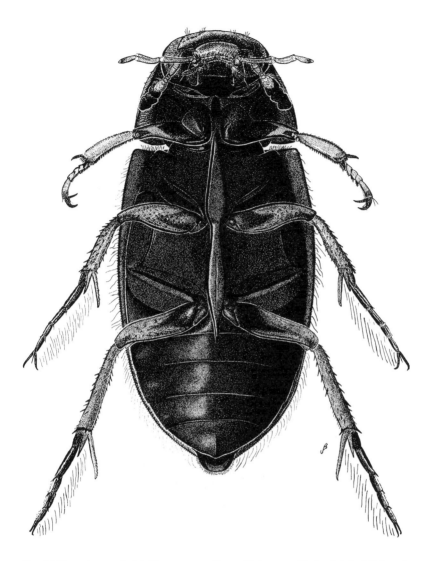

Fig. 87. Ventral view of adult *Tropisternus sublaevis* (Coleoptera: Hydrophilidae) (13 mm).

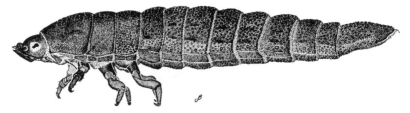

Fig. 88. Lateral view of a *Heterlimnius corpulentus* larva (Coleoptera: Elmidae) (5 mm).
From Ward (1992a), *Aquatic Insect Ecology*. Copyright © 1992 by John Wiley and Sons
Inc. Reprinted by permission of John Wiley and Sons Inc.

Fig. 89. Dorsal view of a *Heterlimnius corpulentus* adult (Coleoptera: Elmidae) (2.5 mm).
From Ward (1992a), *Aquatic Insect Ecology*. Copyright © 1992 by John Wiley and Sons
Inc. Reprinted by permission of John Wiley and Sons Inc.

DIPTERA

The Diptera, or true flies, include a highly diverse assemblage of terrestrial and aquatic insects characterized by only one pair of functional wings in the adult stage. The immatures of aquatic species occur in virtually all freshwater habitat types. Dipterans, mayflies, stoneflies, caddisflies, and elmid beetles collectively often constitute 90 percent or more of the total benthic macroinvertebrates in Colorado mountain streams. The adults of aquatic dipterans are terrestrial, the larvae aquatic. The pupae of some groups (e.g., mosquitoes and midges) remain in the water, whereas others (e.g., most crane flies) pupate on land. The larvae of aquatic dipterans exhibit all major food habits and feeding mechanisms. Dipterans undergo three or four larval instars. Although larval dipterans lack true jointed legs, fleshy protuberances (prolegs) may be present on one or more segments. Some species produce several generations per year, whereas others require several years to complete a single generation. Some aquatic dipterans are widely used as indicators of eutrophication and pollution. Others are pests of humans and domestic animals or serve as disease vectors. Volume 1 of the *Manual of Nearctic Diptera* (McAlpine et al. 1981) treats all the families considered herein except Syrphidae and Muscidae, which are treated in Volume 2 (McAlpine et al. 1987). Very little work has been conducted on Colorado aquatic dipterans, especially stream forms. The following larval key includes, but is not limited to, the families commonly encountered in Colorado mountain streams.

KEY TO COLORADO FAMILIES OF LARVAL DIPTERA

1. Mandibles moving against each other in a horizontal or oblique plane; larvae with a distinct, exposed head capsule, except retracted in Tipulidae..2

   Mandibles moving parallel to each other in a vertical plane; head capsule variously reduced and partially or completely retracted within thorax..10

2. Head partially or completely retracted within thorax, heavily sclerotized only anteriorly; one to three pairs of hair-fringed lobes at posterior end (Fig. 103)......................Tipulidae (p. 141)

   Head capsule complete and exposed; usually without posterior hair; fringed lobes..3

3. Head not clearly separated from thorax; body of six divisions, each with a ventral sucker (Fig. 90)....................Blephariceridae (p. 142)

    Head clearly separated from thorax; body not divided into six divisions..4

4. Six pairs of large abdominal prolegs, circlets of hooks at apices; antennae forked (Fig. 91)......................Deuterophlebiidae (p. 143)

    Prolegs, if present, on no more than three abdominal segments; antennae not forked..5

5. Paired ventral prolegs on abdominal segments 1 and sometimes 2 (not shown in dorsal view in Fig. 94); two flattened lobes with marginal hair fringes at end of abdomen................Dixidae (p. 143)

    Abdomen without prolegs (may have thoracic or anal prolegs); without flattened hair-fringed lobes at end of abdomen.......................6

6. Prothorax with one proleg; head with a pair of cephalic fans; terminal abdominal segments swollen; end of abdomen with a circlet of hooks (Fig. 92)...Simuliidae (p. 143)

    Prothorax lacking prolegs, or with a pair of ventral prolegs; without cephalic fans; posterior portion of abdomen not conspicuously swollen and lacking a circlet of hooks...7

7. Prothorax without prolegs...8

    Prothorax with paired prolegs; paired anal prolegs present; gills present or absent (Fig. 108)..........................Chironomidae (p. 144)

8. Long filaments projecting from abdomen (Fig. 93)......Tanyderidae (p. 145)

    Abdomen without projecting filaments..9

9. Body with dorsal sclerotized plates; a short, conical respiratory tube at end of abdomen (Fig. 98)..............................Psychodidae (p. 146)

    Body without dorsal sclerotized plates; without conical respiratory tube; body may be extremely elongated, almost needlelike (Fig. 96).....
    ....Ceratopogonidae (p. 146)

10. Sclerotized portions of head capsule exposed externally..............11

    External sclerotized portions of head capsule absent, head reduced and entirely within thorax...13

11. Body somewhat flattened; calcium deposits give body surface a crystalline appearance (Fig. 97)............................Stratiomyidae (p. 146)

Larvae not conspicuously flattened; body surface without calcium deposits..12

12. Seven pairs of abdominal prolegs; terminal abdominal segment bearing two pointed, hair-fringed lobes; tubercles projecting from most abdominal segments (Fig. 95)............................Athericidae (p. 146)

Seven or eight pairs of abdominal prolegs; terminal abdominal segment with one to four rounded lobes bearing setae; tubercles absent (Fig. 99)...Empididae (p. 147)

13. Single respiratory tube present; mouth hooks absent (Fig. 101)...Syrphidae (p. 147)

Without single respiratory tube; mouth hooks present (Fig. 102)...Muscidae (p. 148)

Family Tipulidae. Larvae of nine genera commonly encountered in Colorado mountain streams are distinguished as follows:

1. Spiracular disc at end of abdomen surrounded by six lobes (Figs. 103, 104)..*Tipula*

Spiracular disc surrounded by five or fewer lobes............................2

2. Spiracles absent; dorsal and lateral lobes of ninth abdominal segment absent or extremely reduced; one or two long ventral lobes.....3

Spiracles present; dorsal and lateral lobes present or absent.........4

3. Two long ventral lobes; long anal gills present; conspicuous dorsal and ventral creeping welts on abdominal segments 2–7.........*Antocha*

A single long ventral lobe projecting from end of abdomen; anal gills short and inconspicuous; without conspicuous creeping welts...*Hesperoconopa*

4. Dorsal and lateral lobes of spiracular disc absent or greatly reduced, ventral lobes elongate..5

Ventral lobes of spiracular disc usually short; if long, then median dorsal and/or lateral lobes are well developed..................................6

5. With long paired prolegs on abdominal segments 3–7.......*Dicranota*

Abdomen without prolegs..*Pedicia*

6. Spiracular disc with four or five lobes..7

Spiracular disc with three lobes or without distinct lobes.............10

7. Internal portion of head well sclerotized dorsally and laterally (if not visible through skin, make an incision alongside of prothorax);

tips of maxillae not visible when head retracted.....*Limonia* (in part)

Internal portion of head composed of elongate, rodlike sclerites; tips of maxilla visible even when head retracted............................8

8. Spiracular disc with five short, bluntly rounded lobes....................
    ....*Rhabdomastix* (in part)

    Lobes of spiracular disc (usually four in number) not all short and bluntly rounded..9

9. With a dark, narrow transverse bar (part of hypopharynx) visible beneath the surface of the mid-ventral region of the head just before the line of attachment of the skin............................*Limnophila*

    Without dark, narrow transverse bar beneath surface of mid-ventral region of head; often with swollen (bulbous) seventh abdominal segment 1..*Hexatoma*

10. Spiracular disc without lobes, with two clawlike projections on ventral margin..*Rhabdomastix* (in part)

    Spiracular disc with two small ventral lobes and a small dorsal lobe; without clawlike projections........................*Limonia* (in part)

This key is modified and greatly simplified from Byers (1996). No suitable species keys are available for larval crane flies. The biology of tipulids is treated by Pritchard (1983). Some larval crane flies inhabit terrestrial soils; others are aquatic. Numerous species inhabit running waters, and some of these reside in mountain streams. Most aquatic larvae breathe atmospheric air and must periodically replenish their air supply at the water surface. Pupation usually occurs on land. Most aquatic species are univoltine. Most larvae are detritivore shredders; others are collector-gatherers. Some of the common genera in Colorado mountains streams (e.g., *Dicranota*, *Hexatoma*) prey on aquatic insects and other invertebrates. Very little ecological data are available for the tipulids of Colorado mountain streams.

Family Blephariceridae. Larvae of the three genera commonly collected from Colorado mountain streams may be separated as follows:

1. Ventral gill tufts of six filaments, arranged in a semicircle in a single plane..*Bibiocephala*

    Ventral gill tufts of three to five or seven to eight filaments, not in a single plane and most pointing anteriolaterally........................2

2. Dorsal pseudopods double, each with a subequal, elongate dorsal branch; or ventral gill tufts with three filaments.................*Philorus*

   Dorsal pseudopods single; ventral gill tufts with five to eight filaments (Fig. 90)...*Agathon*

Hogue (1987) provides keys to all stages of blepharicerids, or net-winged midges, occurring in Colorado. The immature stages are restricted to rapidly flowing streams. Larvae occur on smooth rock surfaces, often in torrential currents. They maintain position by attaching to the substrate surface using the six hydraulic suckers located on the ventral surface. Larvae feed by scraping algae from rocks.

Family Deuterophlebiidae. This family, the mountain midges, contains a single genus, *Deuterophlebia.* Only *D. coloradensis* (Fig. 91) occurs in Colorado (Courtney 1990). Immature stages are restricted to mountain streams. Larvae inhabit the upper surfaces of rocks in rapid current. Larvae feed by scraping algae from rock surfaces. Courtney (1991) reviews the life histories of these fascinating flies.

Family Dixidae. Dixid midges are occasionally collected from Colorado mountain streams. The larvae (Fig. 94) are aquatic; pupation occurs a short distance above the water level. *Dixa* is the most common genus in Colorado mountain streams. Peters and Cook (1966) treat the Nearctic dixids; Nowell (1951) deals with the western North American fauna. Little is known of the ecology of dixid midges. The mouth brushes are apparently used to collect food from substrate surfaces or to filter particles from the current.

Family Simuliidae. Three genera are known to occur in Colorado mountain streams. Larvae are distinguished as follows:

1. Tips of secondary cephalic fan (beneath primary fan), when expanded, forming a straight line; antennal segments 1 and 2 colorless, 3 and 4 darkly pigmented; median tooth of submentum trifid.....*Prosimulium*

   Tips of secondary cephalic fan forming an arc when expanded; antennal segments 1 and 2 yellow to brown, 3 and 4 rarely dark brown; median tooth of submentum single...2

2. Hypostoma with median tooth and outer lateral teeth of each side moderately large and subequal in height, with three smaller, equal sublateral teeth on each side...*Simulium*

Hypostoma with uniformly small teeth, with outer lateral and sublateral teeth directed anteromedially..............................*Metacnephia*

Peterson and Kondratieff (1994) review the black flies occurring in Colorado, providing keys to larvae, pupae, and adults. Larvae are restricted to running waters. The larvae spin a mat of silk on the substrate to which they attach their posterior circlet of hooks. The cephalic fans are used to filter fine suspended particles from the water column. Mature larvae spin a pupal case (Fig. 92); the pupal stage normally lasts one week or less. The females of many species require a blood meal to complete egg maturation; they are serious pests of humans and other warm-blooded animals in some regions. In Colorado, *Prosimulium* extends to higher elevations than *Simulium*, the latter being characteristic of streams at middle and lower elevations. Several species of *Prosimulium* constituted a major part of the benthic fauna in the alpine segment of a Colorado stream (Elgmork and Saether 1970).

Family Chironomidae. Despite their abundance, diversity, and presumed ecological importance, extremely little work has been conducted on the chironomids (true midges) of Colorado mountain streams. Detailed work on larval stages has been restricted to a few studies on limited segments of specific lotic systems (Saether 1970; Shoutis 1981; Dodson in Peckarsky, Dodson, and Conklin 1985; Ruse, Herrmann, and Sublette 2000). Because of the paucity of data, it is not possible to develop even a provisional key to the chironomid genera of Colorado mountain streams. The following key (after Mason 1973) distinguishes the five North American subfamilies, all of which occur in Colorado:

1. Fork-shaped ligula present (Fig. 105), antennae retractile..............
....Tanypodinae

   Ligula lacking, antennae nonretractile............................2
2. Premandibles absent.................................Podonominae

   Premandibles present (Fig. 106)..3
3. Paralabial plates present, surface with striations (Fig. 106)............
....Chironominae

   Paralabial plates present or absent; if present, surface without striations but may be wrinkled or bear hairs (Fig. 107)..........................4

4. Third segment of antennae annulated (Fig. 106)..............Diamesinae

Third segment of antennae without annulations......Orthocladiinae

Identification of chironomid larvae is a relatively tedious and arduous task. The head (ventral side up) and the body should be mounted separately on a microscope slide. Many key characteristics are based on minute details requiring a phase contrast microscope. See Coffman and Ferrington (1996) for more detailed instructions on the preparation of specimens for identification. At least initially, one should use identification manuals such as Mason (1973), Simpson and Bode (1980), or Epler (1995) that contain illustrations or micrographs of key characters. Simpson and Bode's (1980) key to the lotic chironomid larvae of New York State and Oliver and Roussel's (1983) key to the genera of larval midges of Canada work relatively well for the Colorado fauna, with the exception of the Diamesinae in the New York treatment. Diamesinae, poorly represented in New York, are an important component of Colorado streams, especially at high elevations. For example, two species of *Diamesa* dominated the fauna in the uppermost part of North Boulder Creek well above treeline (Elgmork and Saether 1970). Doughman's (1983) guide to Nearctic Diamesinae includes keys for the identification of larvae. Generic keys for the entire North American chironomid fauna (larvae and pupae) have been prepared by Coffman and Ferrington (1996). Generic keys for Holarctic larvae and pupae are available in Wiederholm (1983, 1986). Additionally, Peckarsky, Dodson, and Conklin (1985) provide keys to genera of chironomid larvae of the streams in the vicinity of Rocky Mountain Biological Laboratory.

Cranston (1995) and Armitage, Cranston, and Pinder (1995) provide much ecological information on this family and should be consulted. Additionally, Hudson et al. (1990) include useful ecological information on many Colorado midge genera. All functional feeding groups are collectively represented by the various species of chironomid larvae. It is clear that chironomids play important roles in the mountain streams of Colorado. It is equally clear that our knowledge of lotic chironomid taxonomy, distribution, and ecology is in an embryonic state.

Family Tanyderidae. From this family of primitive crane flies, a single species, *Protanyderus margarita*, occurs in Colorado. The larvae and pupae are described by Knight (1963, 1964). Larvae (Fig. 93) burrow in stream segments where sand is intermixed with rubble or gravel. The species is rarely encountered in Colorado, but is probably widespread in lower-elevation mountain streams.

Family Psychodidae. Larvae of the two genera of moth flies commonly encountered in Colorado mountain streams are distinguished as follows:

1. Larvae cylindrical; without ventral suckers (Fig. 98)............*Pericoma*

    Larvae dorsoventrally flattened; several ventral suckerlike discs present...*Maruina*

    The immatures of some aquatic species of psychodids are characteristic of waters high in organic matter, including polluted streams. *Maruina* and *Pericoma*, however, inhabit pristine mountain streams. These genera are collector-gatherers or scrapers.

Family Ceratopogonidae. Larvae of biting midges are occasionally collected from Colorado mountain streams. The immatures of most species inhabit standing waters or are semiaquatic. Most larvae collected from Colorado mountain streams are needlelike in shape and lack prolegs (Fig. 96), as do species of *Palpomyia*, one of the few genera occurring in lotic habitats (Merritt and Cummins 1996). Pennak (1978) provides generic keys to known ceratopogonid larvae. Most aquatic species are predators or collector-gatherers.

Family Stratiomyidae. Larvae (Fig. 97) of the two genera of soldier flies that are most likely to be encountered in Colorado mountain streams are separated as follows:

1. With a pair of ventral hooks on seventh abdominal segment......
    ....*Euparyphus*

    Without ventral hooks on seventh abdominal segment.....*Stratiomys*

    There are no suitable species keys for larvae. McFadden (1967) provides a review of North American larvae. The larvae of aquatic soldier flies occur in a variety of habitats, including hot springs and highly saline waters. Most aquatic species are collector-gatherers or scrapers.

Family Athericidae. Only a single species, *Atherix pachypus*, of this family is known to occur in the West and Colorado (Webb 1977). The larvae (Fig. 95) are common in Colorado mountain streams. Eggs are deposited on objects above the water surface. Upon hatching, the larvae fall into the water. Larvae have piercing mouthparts and prey upon chironomids, mayflies, and other aquatic insects. Pupation occurs above the edge of the water.

Family Empididae. Larvae of the three genera of dance flies commonly encountered in Colorado mountain streams are separated as follows:

1. Seven pairs of abdominal prolegs; terminal abdominal segment rounded, without prominent caudal lobes, at most with small dorsal and apical tubercles bearing setae..................................*Chelifera*

    Seven or eight pairs of abdominal prolegs; terminal abdominal segment with prominent caudal lobes..2

2. Seven pairs of abdominal prolegs; terminal abdominal segment with a single, but somewhat medially divided, apical lobe......*Hemerodromia*

    Eight pairs of abdominal prolegs; terminal abdominal segment with two dorsolateral lobes and a central lobe that is either somewhat divided medially or appears as two separate lobes that are shorter than the dorsolateral lobes (central lobe[s] not visible in Fig. 99).......*Clinocera*

There are no suitable species keys to immature stages. Steyskal and Knutson (1981) provide generic keys to known Nearctic larvae (from which the preceding key was adapted) and pupae. Pupae of *Chelifera* and *Hemerodromia* (Fig. 100) have long filaments (spiracular gills) projecting from the sides of the body, but such filaments are absent from *Chelifera*. A recent paper by MacDonald and Harkrider (1999) indicated that there is no definite association for Nearctic *Chelifera* larvae, making generic identification somewhat tentative. Larvae of most aquatic species are predaceous on other aquatic insects. Harper (1980) conducted a study of the distribution and emergence of dance flies in a watershed in Quebec. He found that most species are univoltine and that certain genera characterize particular lotic habitats.

Family Syrphidae. The flower flies are not typical inhabitants of mountain streams. They are included because the larvae of a few species are adapted to low-oxygen waters and thus characterize organically polluted streams. Larvae of *Eristalis*, the only common truly aquatic member of the family, are called "rat-tailed maggots" because of the telescopic caudal respiratory tube (Fig. 101). The larvae are able to feed on decaying organic matter in shallow water devoid of oxygen by breathing atmospheric air inhaled through the elongated respiratory tube.

Family Muscidae. *Lispoides* (= *Limnophora*) *aequifrons* (Fig. 102) is the only species from this family known to occur in Colorado mountain streams. The larvae are predators of aquatic insects and other macroinvertebrates.

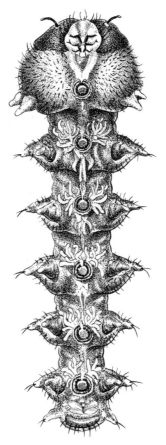

Fig. 90. Ventral view of an *Agathon elegantula* larva (Diptera: Blephariceridae) (11 mm). From Ward (1992a), *Aquatic Insect Ecology*. Copyright © 1992 by John Wiley and Sons Inc. Reprinted by permission of John Wiley and Sons Inc.

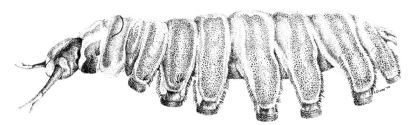

Fig. 91. Lateral view of a *Deuterophlebia coloradensis* larvae (Diptera: Deuterophlebiidae) (3mm). From Ward (1992a), *Aquatic Insect Ecology*. Copyright © 1992 by John Wiley and Sons Inc. Reprinted by permission of John Wiley and Sons Inc.

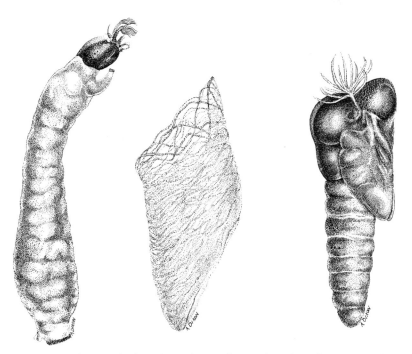

Fig. 92. Lateral views of a larva (7 mm), pupa (4.5 mm), and pupal case of *Simulium arcticum* (Diptera: Simuliidae). From Ward (1992a), *Aquatic Insect Ecology*. Copyright © 1992 by John Wiley and Sons Inc. Reprinted by permission of John Wiley and Sons Inc.

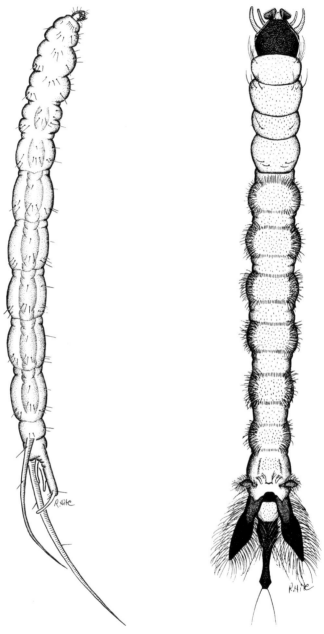

Fig. 93. Lateral view of a *Protanyderus margarita* larva (Diptera: Tanyderidae) (13 mm).

Fig. 94. Dorsal view of a *Dixa* sp. larva (Diptera: Dixidae) (6 mm).

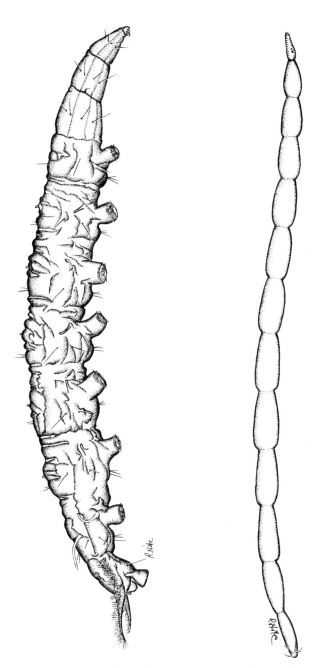

Fig. 95. Lateral view if an *Atherix pachypus*
larva (Diptera: Athericidae) (20 mm)

Fig. 96. Lateral view of a ceratopogonid
larva (Diptera: Ceratopogonidae) (9 mm).

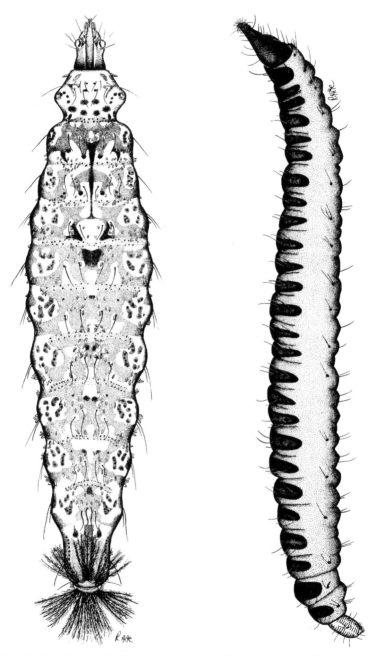

Fig. 97. Dorsal view of a *Euparyphus* sp. larva (Diptera: Stratiomyidae) (12 mm).

Fig. 98. Lateral view of a *Pericoma* sp. larva (Diptera: Psychodidae) (6 mm).

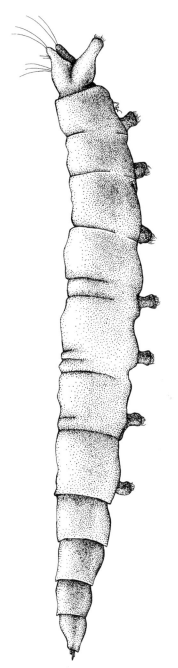

Fig. 99. Lateral view of a *Clinocera* sp. larva (Diptera: Empididae) (4 mm).

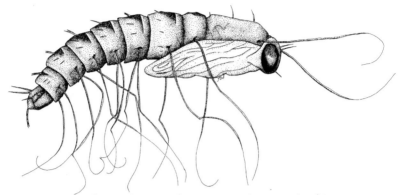

Fig. 100. Lateral view of a *Hemerodromia* sp. pupa (Diptera: Empididae) (4 mm).

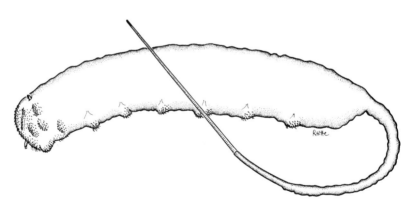

Fig. 101. Lateral view of an *Eristalis* sp. larva (Diptera: Syrphidae) (17 mm excluding the respiratory tube).

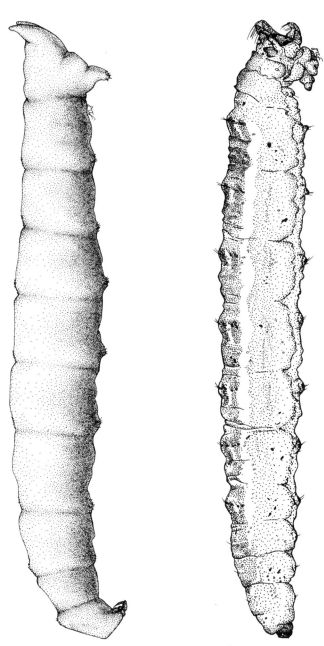

Fig. 102. Lateral view of a *Lispoides aequifrons* larva (Diptera: Muscidae) (12 mm).

Fig. 103. Lateral view of a *Tipula* sp. larva (Diptera: Tipulidae) (52 mm).

Fig. 104. Spiracular disc of a *Tipula* sp. larva. The lobes of the spiracular disc are outlined with dark lines. The two circles are the spiracles. Anal gills are shown ventral to the spiracular disc.

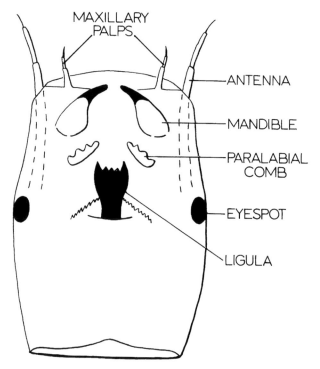

Fig. 105. Ventral view (diagrammatic) of the larval head capsule of a Tanypodinae (Diptera: Chironomidae).

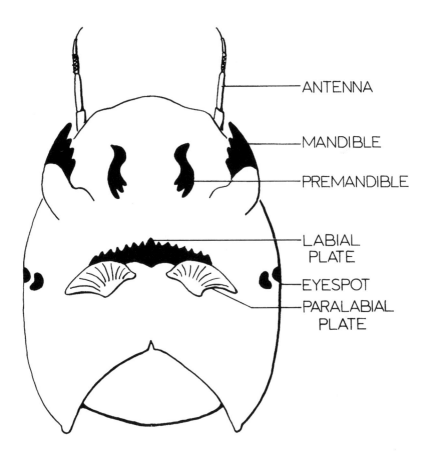

ANTENNA

MANDIBLE

PREMANDIBLE

LABIAL PLATE

EYESPOT

PARALABIAL PLATE

Fig. 106. Ventral view (diagrammatic) of a larval head capsule with composite features of Diamesinae, Orthocladiinae, and Chironominae (Diptera: Chironomidae).

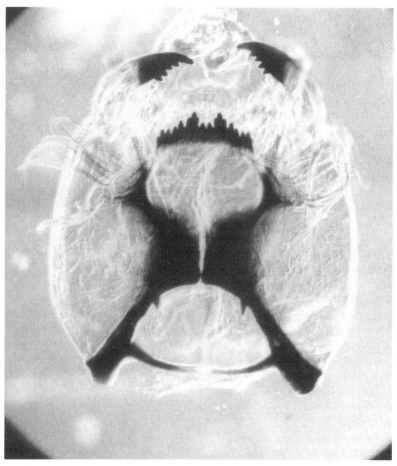

Fig. 107. Photomicrograph of the ventral surface of a *Prodiamesa olivacea* head capsule (Diptera: Chironomidae) (photo by J. V. Ward).

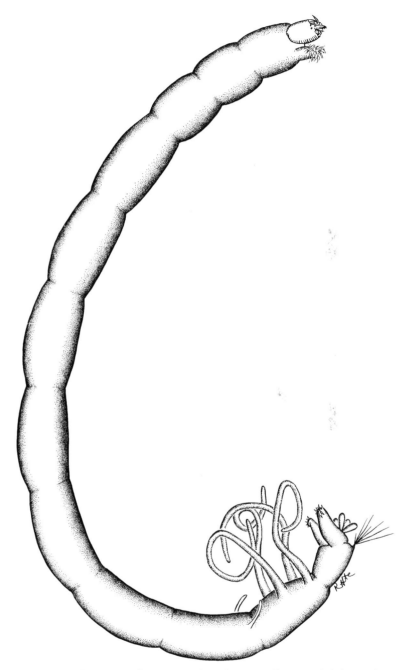

Fig. 108. Lateral view of a *Chironomus* sp. larva (Diptera: Chironomidae) (25 mm).

OTHER ORDERS

The remaining orders of aquatic insects (Odonata, Hemiptera, Lepidoptera, and Megaloptera) are poorly represented in Colorado mountain streams. The aquatic members of these orders primarily inhabit ponds, slow streams, or the littoral zone of lakes. The Odonata (dragonflies and damselflies), a well-known group of aquatic insects, are rarely encountered in Colorado mountain streams. The dragonfly *Ophiogomphus severus* (Fig. 109) is the only member of the order known to occur in high-gradient mountain streams of Colorado. Only in riverine reaches or special habitats such as spring brooks are additional species of Odonata normally encountered in running waters. Two suborders of Odonata occur in Colorado. Anisoptera or dragonfly nymphs are robust and respire by means of gills lining the rectal chamber. Zygoptera or damselfly nymphs are more slender and possess three leaflike caudal gills (Fig. 110). Nymphs of both suborders are voracious predators. The modified labium (mask), normally held under the head (Fig. 110), can be thrust forward to capture prey organisms. Needham, Westfall, and May (2000) and Westfall and May (1996) provide species keys to most nymphal dragonflies and damselflies of North America, respectively. Corbet (1999) recently provided a magnificent review of the biology of the order. A species list and county distributions for the Odonata of Colorado are provided by Evans (1988, 1995).

The order Megaloptera includes the families Sialidae (alderflies) and Corydalidae (dobsonflies and fishflies). The larvae of these families are separated as follows:

1. With eight pairs of lateral abdominal filaments; anal prolegs at apex of abdomen (Fig. 111) ....Corydalidae, *Corydalus*

   With seven pairs of lateral abdominal filaments; without anal prolegs; a long pointed filament at apex of abdomen.......Sialidae, *Sialis*

Most of the records for the single Colorado species, *Sialis velata* (Sialidae), are from the eastern portion of the state; however, this species has been collected from the Yampa River basin and a tributary of the Poudre River, Larimer County. *Corydalus texanus* (Corydalidae) (Fig. 111) is one of the largest aquatic insects; mature larvae may reach 8 cm in length. Larvae reside under large rocks in riverine reaches where they prey upon aquatic insects and other macroinvertebrates. It appears that in Colorado this species is limited to the Purgatoire River on the Eastern Slope and the Colorado River and its tributaries on the Western Slope (Herrmann and Davis 1991; Contreras-Ramos 1998). Megalopterans do not occur in high-gradient Colorado mountain streams.

Lepidoptera (butterflies and moths) is a primarily terrestrial order of insects, although several families of moths contain aquatic or semi-aquatic representatives. Most truly aquatic species are in the family Pyralidae, which also includes terrestrial insects such as corn borers. With few exceptions, aquatic moth larvae are associated with aquatic vascular plants, thus restricting them to ponds, slow-moving streams, or the littoral zone of lakes. Several species of *Petrophila* reside in relatively rapid streams. The larvae live under silk canopies constructed on the surfaces of rocks from which they scrape algae. *Petrophila avernalis* occurs commonly in the Poudre River and its larger tributaries. A dense population of *P. longipennis* was discovered in a rocky section of a plains stream (Ward, unpublished data), but only occasionally have species of *Petrophila* been reported from Colorado mountain streams.

Members of the order Hemiptera (true bugs) are largely terrestrial. Surface bugs, such as water striders, are not considered herein. Along with beetles, the aquatic bugs include species that are truly aquatic in both immature and adult stages. Most aquatic hemipterans are associated with well-vegetated lentic and slow-flowing lotic habitats. There are few records of truly aquatic bugs from Colorado mountain streams. A few species occur in riverine reaches, but most of these are lentic forms that are also able to reside in certain river habitats, such as several Corixidae (water boatmen, especially *Sigara alternata* and *S. grossolineata*). A notable exception is the naucorid bug *Ambrysus mormon* (Fig. 112), which prefers well-oxygenated running waters with gravel or rocky bottoms (Usinger 1956). Nymphs and adults are predators, piercing their prey with the typical hemipteran beak. *Ambrysus mormon* has been collected from the Yampa, White, and San Juan River basins in Colorado.

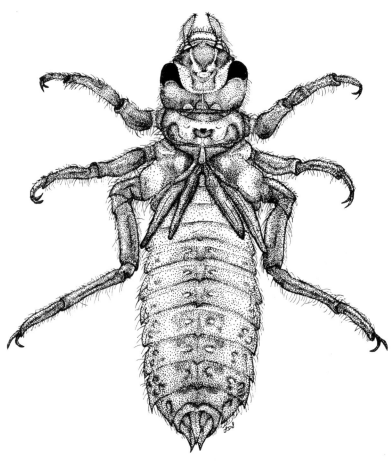

Fig. 109. Dorsal view of an *Ophiogomphus severus* nymph (Odonata: Anisoptera) (25 mm).

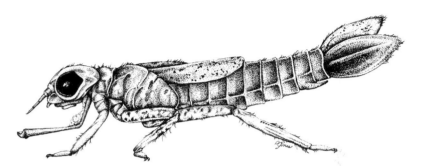

Fig. 110. Lateral view of an *Argia* sp. nymph (Odonata: Zygoptera) (12 mm).

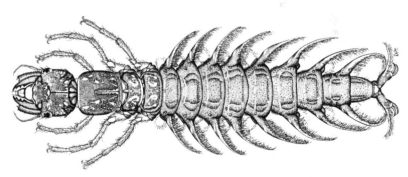

Fig. 111. Dorsal view of a *Corydalus texanus* larva (Megaloptera: Corydalidae) (54 mm). From Ward (1992a), *Aquatic Insect Ecology*. Copyright © 1992 by John Wiley and Sons Inc. Reprinted by permission of John Wiley and Sons Inc.

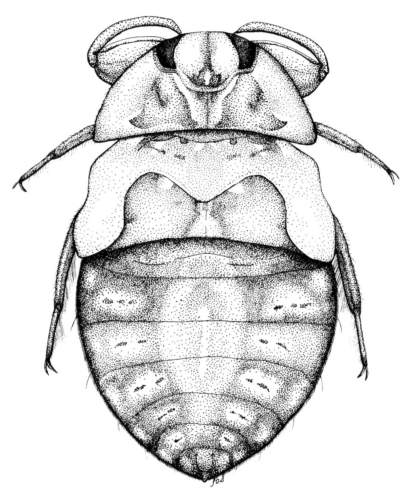

Fig. 112. Dorsal view of an *Ambrysus mormon* nymph (Hemiptera: Naucoridae) (10 mm).

APPENDIX A

Recorded Colorado distributions of mountain stream mayflies (Ephemeroptera) by major drainage basin.

Family				Drainage Basin						
Species	SP	NP	YR	WR	CR	DR	SJ	RG	SL	AR
AMELETIDAE										
Ameletus celer	X	X	—	—	X	—	—	—	—	—
Ameletus doddsianus	X	X	—	—	X	—	—	—	X	—
Ameletus sparsatus	X	X	—	—	X	—	—	X	—	—
Ameletus subnotatus	X	X	X	—	X	—	—	—	—	—
Ameletus validus	X	—	—	—	X	—	—	X	—	—
Ameletus velox	—	—	—	—	X	—	—	X	X	—
AMETROPODIDAE										
Ametropus albrighti	—	—	—	X	—	—	—	—	—	—
BAETIDAE										
Acentrella insignificans	X	X	X	X	X	X	X	X	X	X
Acentrella parvulum	X	—	X	—	—	—	—	—	—	—
Acentrella turbida	X	X	X	—	X	—	X	X	—	X

continued on next page

Family / Species				Drainage Basin						
	SP	NP	YR	WR	CR	DR	SJ	RG	SL	AR
BAETIDAE (continued)										
Acerpenna pygmaea	—	—	X	—	—	—	—	—	—	—
Baetis bicaudatus	X	X	X	X	X	X	X	X	X	X
Baetis flavistriga	X	X	X	—	X	—	—	X	—	X
Baetis magnus	X	—	—	—	X	—	—	—	—	X
Baetis notos	X	—	—	X	X	—	X	X	X	X
Baetis tricaudatus	X	X	X	X	X	X	X	X	X	X
Callibaetis ferrugineus hageni	X	X	X	X	X	X	X	X	X	X
Callibaetis pallidus	X	—	—	—	X	—	—	X	—	X
Callibaetis pictus	X	—	—	—	X	—	—	—	—	X
Camelobaetidius kickapoo	—	—	X	—	—	—	—	—	—	—
Camelobaetidius warreni	X	—	X	—	X	—	—	—	—	—
Centroptilum bifurcatum	X	X	X	—	X	—	X	—	X	X
Diphetor hageni	X	X	—	—	X	—	X	X	—	X
Fallceon quilleri	X	—	X	X	X	X	X	X	X	—
Heterocloeon frivolum	—	X	—	—	—	—	—	—	—	—
Plauditus virilis	X	X	X	—	—	—	—	X	—	—
Procloeon album	—	X	—	—	—	—	—	—	—	—
Pseudocloeon dardanum	X	—	X	X	X	—	—	—	—	—
CAENIDAE										
Brachycercus tuberculatus	—	—	X	—	X	—	—	—	—	—
Caenis amica	X	X	X	X	X	X	X	X	X	X
Caenis bajaensis	X	—	—	—	—	—	—	—	—	—
Caenis latipennis	X	—	—	—	—	—	—	—	—	—
Caenis youngi	—	X	—	—	—	—	—	—	—	—
EPHEMERELLIDAE										
Attenella margarita	X	X	X	X	X	X	X	X	X	—
Drunella coloradensis	X	X	X	—	X	X	X	X	—	X
Drunella doddsi	X	X	X	X	X	X	X	X	X	X
Drunella grandis	X	X	X	X	X	X	X	X	—	X
Ephemerella aurivillii	—	X	—	—	—	—	—	—	—	—
Ephemerella inermis	X	—	X	X	X	X	X	—	—	X
Ephemerella infrequens	X	X	X	—	X	—	—	X	—	X
Serratella micheneri	X	X	X	—	X	—	—	X	—	—
Serratella tibialis	X	X	X	—	X	—	—	X	X	X
Timpanoga hecuba	X	X	X	X	X	X	X	X	X	X
EPHEMERIDAE										
Ephemera simulans	—	X	X	—	—	—	—	—	X	X
HEPTAGENIIDAE										
Cinygmula mimus	X	X	—	—	X	—	—	X	—	X
Cinygmula par	X	X	X	—	—	—	—	X	—	—
Cinygmula ramaleyi	X	X	X	—	X	—	—	X	—	X
Cinygmula tarda	—	—	—	—	—	—	—	—	—	—
Epeorus albertae	X	X	X	—	X	—	—	X	—	X

continued on next page

Family Species	SP	NP	YR	WR	CR	DR	SJ	RG	SL	AR
HEPTAGENIIDAE (continued)										
Epeorus deceptivus	X	X	X	—	X	X	X	X	—	X
Epeorus longimanus	X	X	X	—	X	X	X	X	—	X
Heptagenia diabasia	X	—	—	—	—	—	—	—	—	—
Heptagenia elegantula	X	X	X	X	X	X	X	X	X	X
Heptagenia solitaria	X	X	X	X	X	X	X	X	X	X
Nixe criddlei	X	X	—	X	—	—	—	X	—	—
Nixe simplicioides	X	X	X	X	X	X	—	X	—	X
Pseudiron centralis	—	—	—	—	X	—	—	—	—	X
Rhithrogena flavianula	—	—	—	—	X	—	—	X	—	—
Rhithrogena hageni	X	X	X	X	X	X	X	X	X	X
Rhithrogena pellucida	—	X	—	—	—	—	—	—	—	—
Rhithrogena robusta	X	X	—	—	X	—	—	X	—	X
Rhithrogena undulata	—	—	X	X	X	—	X	X	—	—
ISONYCHIIDAE										
Isonychia campestris	—	—	X	X	X	—	—	—	—	—
Isonychia rufa	X	—	—	—	—	—	—	—	—	X
LEPTOHYPHIDAE										
Asioplax corpulentus	—	—	X	—	X	—	—	—	—	—
Asioplax edmundsi	—	—	X	—	X	—	—	—	—	—
Tricorythodes minutus	X	X	X	X	X	X	X	X	X	X
LEPTOPHLEBIIDAE										
Choroterpes albiannulata	—	—	X	X	—	—	—	—	—	—
Choroterpes inornata	X	X	—	—	X	—	—	X	X	—
Leptophlebia cupida	X	X	X	—	—	—	—	—	—	—
Leptophlebia nebulosa	X	—	—	—	X	—	—	—	—	—
Neochoroterpes oklahoma	—	—	—	—	—	—	—	—	—	X
Paraleptophlebia bicornuta	—	—	X	—	—	—	—	—	—	—
Paraleptophlebia debilis	X	X	X	X	—	X	—	—	—	—
Paraleptophlebia heteronea	X	X	X	X	—	X	—	X	—	—
Paraleptophlebia memorialis	X	X	—	—	X	—	—	—	—	—
Paraleptophlebia packi	—	X	X	X	X	—	—	—	—	—
Traverella albertana	—	—	X	X	X	—	—	—	—	—
OLIGONEURIIDAE										
Lachlania saskatchewanensis	—	—	X	X	X	—	—	—	—	X
POLYMITARCYIDAE										
Ephoron album	X	X	X	X	X	X	—	—	—	—
SIPHLONURIDAE										
Siphlonurus occidentalis	X	X	X	X	X	X	X	X	X	X

Legend: SP = South Platte; NP = North Platte; YR = Yampa River; WR = White River; CR = Colorado River; DR = Dolores River; SJ = San Juan; RG = Rio Grande; SL = San Luis; AR = Arkansas River.

Note: Some distribution records are based on unpublished data from the research laboratory of the authors.

APPENDIX B

Recorded Colorado distributions of mountain stream stoneflies (Plecoptera) by major drainage basin.

Family				Drainage Basins						
Species	SP	NP	YR	WR	CR	DR	SJ	RG	SL	AR
CAPNIIDAE										
Bolshecapnia milami	—	—	—	—	X	—	—	—	—	X
Capnia arapahoe	X	—	—	—	—	—	—	—	—	—
Capnia coloradensis	X	X	X	X	X	X	X	X	—	X
Capnia confusa	X	X	X	X	X	X	X	X	X	X
Capnia decepta	X	—	—	—	—	—	—	—	—	—
Capnia gracilaria	X	X	X	X	X	—	X	X	—	X
Capnia nana	—	—	—	—	X	—	X	X	—	—
Capnia uintahi	—	—	—	X	—	—	—	—	—	—
Capnia vernalis	X	X	X	X	X	X	X	X	—	X
Capnura fibula	—	—	—	—	—	—	—	—	—	X
Capnura wanica	X	—	—	X	—	—	—	—	—	—
Eucapnopsis brevicauda	X	X	X	—	—	—	—	X	—	X
Isocapnia crinita	—	—	—	—	X	—	—	X	—	—

continued on next page

Family Species	SP	NP	YR	WR	CR	DR	SJ	RG	SL	AR
					Drainage Basin					
CAPNIIDAE (continued)										
Isocapnia grandis	—	—	—	—	X	—	—	X	—	—
Isocapnia hyalita	—	—	—	—	—	—	—	X	—	X
Isocapnia vedderensis	—	—	—	—	—	—	X	—	—	—
Paracapnia angulata	X	X	—	—	X	—	—	—	—	—
Utacapnia lemoniana	—	—	X	—	—	—	—	—	—	—
Utacapnia logana	X	X	X	X	X	—	X	—	—	X
Utacapnia poda	—	—	X	—	X	—	X	X	—	—
CHLOROPERLIDAE										
Alloperla pilosa	X	—	—	—	X	—	X	X	—	—
Alloperla severa	—	—	X	—	X	—	—	—	—	—
Plumiperla diversa	X	X	X	—	X	X	X	X	—	X
Suwallia lineosa	—	—	—	—	X	—	—	—	—	—
Suwallia pallidula	X	X	X	—	X	—	X	X	—	X
Suwallia starki	X	X	X	—	X	—	—	X	—	X
Suwallia wardi	X	—	—	—	—	—	—	X	—	X
Sweltsa albertensis	X	—	—	—	X	—	—	—	—	—
Sweltsa borealis	X	X	X	—	X	X	X	X	—	X
Sweltsa coloradensis	X	X	X	X	X	X	X	X	X	X
Sweltsa fidelis	X	X	—	—	X	—	—	X	—	—
Sweltsa lamba	X	X	X	—	X	—	X	X	X	X
Triznaka pintada	X	X	X	—	X	—	X	—	—	X
Triznaka signata	X	X	X	X	X	X	X	X	X	X
LEUCTRIDAE										
Paraleuctra jewetti	—	—	—	—	X	—	—	—	—	—
Paraleuctra occidentalis	X	X	—	—	X	—	—	X	—	—
Paraleuctra projecta	—	—	—	—	X	—	—	—	—	—
Paraleuctra vershina	X	X	X	X	X	X	X	X	X	X
Perlomyia utahensis	X	—	X	—	X	—	—	—	—	—
NEMOURIDAE										
Amphinemura banksi	X	X	X	X	X	X	X	X	X	X
Malenka californica	X	—	X	—	X	—	—	—	—	X
Malenka coloradensis	X	—	X	—	X	—	X	X	X	X
Malenka flexura	X	—	X	—	X	—	—	X	—	—
Podmosta decepta	X	X	X	—	X	—	—	—	—	—
Podmosta delicatula	X	X	—	—	X	X	X	X	—	X
Prostoia besametsa	X	X	X	X	X	X	X	X	—	X
Zapada cinctipes	X	X	X	X	X	X	X	X	X	X
Zapada frigida	X	—	—	—	X	—	X	X	—	X
Zapada haysi	X	X	—	—	X	X	—	X	—	X
Zapada oregonensis	X	—	—	—	X	—	X	X	—	X
PERLIDAE										
Acroneuria abnormis	—	—	X	X	X	—	X	—	—	—
Claassenia sabulosa	X	X	X	X	X	X	X	X	—	X

continued on next page

| Family | | | | Drainage Basin | | | | | | |
Species	SP	NP	YR	WR	CR	DR	SJ	RG	SL	AR
PERLIDAE (continued)										
Hesperoperla pacifica	X	X	X	X	X	X	X	X	—	X
Perlesta decipiens	X	—	—	—	—	—	—	X	—	—
PERLODIDAE										
Arcynopteryx compacta	X	—	—	—	X	—	—	—	—	—
Cultus aestivalis	X	X	X	X	X	—	X	—	—	X
Diura knowltoni	X	X	—	—	X	—	—	X	—	X
Isogenoides colubrinus	—	—	X	—	X	—	X	X	—	—
Isogenoides elongatus	X	X	X	—	X	—	X	—	X	—
Isogenoides zionensis	—	—	—	—	—	—	X	X	—	—
Isoperla fulva	X	X	X	—	X	X	X	X	—	X
Isoperla longiseta	—	—	X	X	X	—	X	X	—	—
Isoperla mormona	—	—	X	X	X	—	X	X	X	X
Isoperla petersoni	X	—	—	—	—	—	—	—	—	—
Isoperla phalerata	X	X	—	—	X	—	—	X	—	—
Isoperla pinta	—	X	X	—	X	—	—	—	—	—
Isoperla quinquepunctata	X	X	X	X	X	X	X	X	X	X
Isoperla sobria	X	X	—	—	X	—	X	X	—	X
Kogotus modestus	X	X	X	—	X	—	X	X	—	X
Megarcys signata	X	X	X	—	X	X	X	X	—	X
Pictetiella expansa	X	—	—	—	X	—	—	—	—	—
Skwala americana	X	X	X	—	X	X	X	X	—	X
PTERONARCYIDAE										
Pteronarcella badia	X	X	X	X	X	X	X	X	X	X
Pteronarcys californica	X	—	X	X	X	X	X	X	X	X
TAENIOPTERYGIDAE										
Doddsia occidentalis	X	X	—	—	X	X	X	X	—	X
Oemopteryx fosketti	—	—	X	—	X	—	—	X	—	—
Taenionema pacificum	—	—	X	—	X	—	—	—	X	—
Taenionema pallidium	X	X	X	—	X	X	X	X	—	X
Taeniopteryx parvula	—	X	—	—	—	—	—	—	—	—
Taenionema uinta	—	X	X	—	—	—	—	—	—	—

Legend: SP = South Platte; NP = North Platte; YR = Yampa River; WR = White River; CR = Colorado River; DR = Dolores River; SJ = San Juan; RG = Rio Grande; SL = San Luis; AR = Arkansas River.

Note: Some distribution records are based on unpublished data from research laboratory of the authors.

APPENDIX C

Recorded Colorado distributions of mountain stream caddisflies (Trichoptera) by major drainage basin.

Family Species	Drainage Basin									
	SP	NP	YR	WR	CR	DR	SJ	RG	SL	AR
APATANIIDAE										
Allomyia gnathos	X	—	—	—	X	—	—	—	—	X
Allomyia tripunctata	X	—	—	—	X	—	—	—	—	X
BRACHYCENTRIDAE										
Amiocentrus aspilus	X	X	X	—	—	—	—	—	—	—
Brachycentrus americanus	X	X	X	X	X	X	X	X	X	X
Brachycentrus occidentalis	X	X	X	—	X	—	—	X	—	X
Micrasema bactro	X	X	—	X	X	—	—	—	—	X
GLOSSOSOMATIDAE										
Agapetus boulderensis	X	X	—	—	X	—	X	X	—	X
Anagapetus debilis	X	—	—	X	X	—	X	X	—	X
Culoptila cantha	—	X	X	—	X	—	X	—	—	—
Culoptila thoracica	X	X	X	—	X	—	X	X	—	X

continued on next page

Family				Drainage Basin						
Species	SP	NP	YR	WR	CR	DR	SJ	RG	SL	AR
GLOSSOSOMATIDAE (continued)										
Glossosoma alascense	X	—	—	—	—	—	—	—	—	—
Glossosoma parvulum	X	X	X	X	X	X	X	X	X	X
Glossosoma ventrale	X	—	—	—	X	—	X	—	—	X
Glossosoma verdona	X	X	—	—	X	—	X	—	—	X
Protoptila coloma	X	X	—	—	X	—	—	—	—	—
Protoptila erotica	—	X	X	—	X	—	—	—	X	—
HELICOPSYCHIDAE										
Helicopsyche borealis	X	X	X	X	X	—	X	—	—	X
HYDROPSYCHIDAE										
Arctopsyche grandis	X	X	X	X	X	X	X	X	—	X
Cheumatopsyche campyla	X	X	X	—	X	—	—	—	—	—
Cheumatopsyche enonis	—	X	X	—	X	—	X	X	—	—
Cheumatopsyche gracilis	X	X	—	—	—	—	—	—	—	—
Cheumatopsyche pettiti	X	X	—	—	X	—	—	—	—	X
Cheumatopsyche speciosa	—	—	X	—	—	—	—	—	—	—
Cheumatopsyche wabasha	—	—	X	—	—	—	—	—	—	—
Hydropsyche alhedra	—	X	—	—	X	—	—	—	—	—
Hydropsyche bidens	—	X	—	—	X	—	—	—	—	—
Hydropsyche bronta	X	—	—	—	—	—	—	—	—	X
Hydropsyche cockerelli	X	X	X	X	X	X	X	X	X	X
Hydropsyche confusa	—	—	—	X	—	—	—	—	—	—
Hydropsyche morosa	X	X	—	—	X	—	—	—	—	—
Hydropsyche occidentalis	X	X	X	X	X	X	X	X	X	X
Hydropsyche oslari	X	X	X	X	X	X	X	X	—	X
Hydropsyche slossonae	X	X	—	—	X	—	—	—	—	—
Parapsyche almota	—	X	—	X	X	—	—	X	—	—
Parapsyche elsis	—	—	—	X	X	—	—	X	—	X
HYDROPTILIDAE										
Agraylea multipunctata	X	X	—	X	X	—	X	—	—	X
Agraylea saltesea	X	—	—	—	—	—	—	—	—	X
Hydroptila ajax	X	X	X	X	X	—	X	X	—	X
Hydroptila angusta	—	—	X	—	—	—	—	—	—	—
Hydroptila arctia	X	X	—	—	X	—	X	—	—	X
Hydroptila argosa	X	X	X	X	X	—	X	X	—	X
Hydroptila consimilis	X	—	—	—	X	—	—	—	—	—
Hydroptila icona	X	—	—	—	X	—	—	—	—	—
Hydroptila pecos	X	—	—	—	—	—	—	—	—	X
Hydroptila rono	X	X	—	—	X	—	—	—	—	X
Hydroptila xera	X	X	—	—	—	—	X	X	—	X
Leucotrichia pictipes	X	X	—	—	X	—	—	—	—	X
Mayatrichia ayma	—	—	—	—	X	—	—	—	—	X
Neotrichia downsi	—	X	—	—	—	—	—	—	—	—

continued on next page

| Family | | | | Drainage | Basin | | | | | |
Species	SP	NP	YR	WR	CR	DR	SJ	RG	SL	AR
HYDROPTILIDAE (continued)										
Neotrichia halia	X	X	X	—	X	—	—	—	—	—
Neotrichia okopa	—	—	X	—	—	—	—	—	—	—
Neotrichia osmena	—	—	—	—	X	—	—	X	—	—
Ochrotrichia logana	X	X	X	X	X	X	X	X	—	X
Ochrotrichia oregona	—	X	—	—	X	—	—	—	—	—
Ochrotrichia stylata	X	X	X	X	X	—	—	X	—	X
Ochrotrichia susanae	—	X	—	—	—	—	—	—	—	X
Oxyethira dualis	X	—	—	—	X	—	—	—	—	X
Stactobiella brustia	X	X	—	—	X	—	X	—	—	—
Stactobiella delira	X	X	—	—	X	—	—	—	—	—
LEPIDOSTOMATIDAE										
Lepidostoma apornum	X	—	—	—	—	—	—	—	—	—
Lepidostoma cascadense	X	X	—	—	X	—	X	X	—	X
Lepidostoma cinereum	—	X	—	—	—	—	—	—	—	—
Lepidostoma ormea	X	X	X	—	X	—	X	X	—	X
Lepidostoma pluviale	X	X	—	—	X	—	—	X	—	X
Lepidostoma roafi	X	X	—	—	X	—	—	X	—	X
Lepidostoma stigma	X	X	—	—	X	—	X	X	—	X
Lepidostoma unicolor	X	X	—	—	X	—	X	X	—	X
LEPTOCERIDAE										
Ceraclea annulicornis	—	—	—	—	X	—	—	—	—	—
Ceraclea arielles	X	X	—	—	X	—	—	—	—	—
Ceraclea cophus	X	—	—	—	X	—	—	—	—	—
Ceraclea maculata	X	—	—	—	—	—	—	—	—	—
Ceraclea resurgens	—	—	X	—	X	—	—	—	—	—
Nectopsyche lahontanensis	X	—	—	—	—	—	—	—	—	—
Nectopsyche stigmatica	X	X	X	—	X	—	—	—	—	—
Oecetis arizonica	—	—	—	—	—	—	X	—	—	—
Oecetis avara	X	X	X	X	X	—	X	X	—	X
Oecetis disjuncta	X	X	—	—	X	—	X	X	—	X
Oecetis inconspicua	X	X	X	X	X	—	X	X	—	X
Ylodes grisea	X	—	—	—	X	—	—	—	—	X
Ylodes reuteri	—	X	—	—	—	—	—	—	—	—
LIMNEPHILIDAE										
Amphicosmoecus canax	X	X	—	—	X	X	X	—	—	X
Anabolia bimaculata	X	X	X	—	X	—	X	X	—	X
Asynarchus nigriculus	X	X	X	—	X	—	—	—	—	X
Chyranda centralis	X	X	—	—	X	—	—	X	—	X
Clistoronia maculata	X	—	—	—	—	—	—	—	—	—
Dicosmoecus atripes	X	X	X	X	X	—	X	X	—	X
Ecclisomyia conspersa	X	—	—	—	X	—	X	—	—	X
Ecclisomyia maculosa	X	—	—	—	X	—	—	X	—	X

continued on next page

Appendix C—continued

| Family | | | | Drainage Basin | | | | | | |
Species	SP	NP	YR	WR	CR	DR	SJ	RG	SL	AR
LIMNEPHILIDAE (continued)										
Glyphopsyche irrorata	X	—	—	—	X	—	—	—	—	—
Hesperophylax consimilis	X	X	—	X	X	X	X	X	—	X
Hesperophylax designatus	X	X	—	X	X	—	—	—	—	—
Hesperophylax magnus	X	—	—	—	—	—	—	—	—	X
Hesperophylax occidentalis	X	X	X	X	X	X	X	X	X	X
Homophylax flavipennis	X	—	—	—	X	—	—	X	—	X
Limnephilus externus	X	X	—	—	X	—	—	X	—	X
Limnephilus frijole	X	—	—	—	—	—	—	—	—	X
Limnephilus lithus	X	—	—	—	—	—	—	—	—	X
Onocosmoecus unicolor	X	X	X	X	X	—	X	X	—	X
Psychoglypha ormiae	X	—	—	—	X	—	—	—	—	—
Psychoglypha subborealis	X	X	—	—	X	—	—	X	—	X
Psychoronia costalis	X	—	—	—	X	—	—	—	—	X
Pycnopsyche guttifer	—	X	X	—	—	—	—	—	—	—
Pycnopsyche subfasciata	X	X	—	—	—	—	—	—	—	—
PHILOPOTAMIDAE										
Chimarra utahensis	X	—	—	—	X	—	—	—	—	X
Dolophilodes aequalis	X	X	X	X	X	—	X	X	—	X
Wormaldia gabriella	X	X	—	—	X	—	—	—	—	—
POLYCENTROPODIDAE										
Polycentropus aureolus	X	X	—	—	X	—	—	—	—	—
Polycentropus cinereus	X	X	X	—	X	—	—	—	—	—
Polycentropus gertschi	—	—	—	—	—	—	X	X	—	—
Polycentropus halidus	—	—	—	—	X	—	—	—	—	—
Polycentropus interruptus	X	—	—	—	—	—	—	—	—	—
Polycentropus variegatus	X	—	—	—	—	—	—	—	—	X
PSYCHOMYIIDAE										
Psychomyia flavida	X	X	X	X	X	—	—	X	X	X
RHYACOPHILIDAE										
Rhyacophila alberta	X	X	—	—	X	—	X	X	—	X
Rhyacophila angelita	X	X	X	X	X	—	X	X	—	X
Rhyacophila bifila	—	X	—	—	—	—	—	—	—	—
Rhyacophila brunnea	X	X	X	X	X	—	X	—	—	X
Rhyacophila coloradensis	X	X	X	X	X	X	X	X	—	X
Rhyacophila harmstoni	X	—	—	—	X	—	—	X	—	X
Rhyacophila hyalinata	X	X	X	—	X	—	X	—	—	X
Rhyacophila nevadensis	X	—	—	—	—	—	—	—	—	—
Rhyacophila pellisa	X	X	X	—	X	X	—	X	—	X
Rhyacophila rotunda	X	—	—	—	X	—	—	—	—	—
Rhyacophila valuma	—	—	—	—	X	—	—	—	—	X
Rhyacophila vao	X	—	—	—	X	—	—	—	—	—
Rhyacophila verrula	X	X	X	—	X	—	X	X	—	X

continued on next page

| Family | | | | Drainage Basin | | | | | | |
Species	SP	NP	YR	WR	CR	DR	SJ	RG	SL	AR
RHYACOPHILIDAE (continued)										
Rhyacophila vocala	—	—	—	—	X	—	—	—	—	—
Rhyacophila vofixa	—	—	—	—	X	—	—	—	—	X
UENOIDAE										
Neothremma alicia	X	—	—	X	X	—	X	X	—	X
Neophylax splendens	X	—	—	X	X	—	—	—	—	—
Oligophlebodes ardis	—	—	X	—	X	—	—	—	—	X
Oligophlebodes minutus	X	X	X	X	X	X	—	X	X	X
Oligophlebodes sierra	—	—	—	—	X	—	—	—	—	—
Oligophlebodes sigma	—	—	—	—	X	—	—	—	—	X

Legend: SP = South Platte; NP = North Platte; YR = Yampa River; WR = White River; CR = Colorado River; DR = Dolores River; SJ = San Juan; RG = Rio Grande; SL = San Luis; AR = Arkansas River.

Note: Some distribution records are based on unpublished data from the research laboratories of David E. Ruiter (Littleton, CO) and authors.

GLOSSARY

Angiosperms	Flowering plants.
Antennal scapes	The basal or first joint or segment of the antennae (see Fig. 51).
Anteromedian	In front and along the midline of the body or a region of the body.
Apex	The uppermost point or tip.
Articulations	Jointed or segmented.
Basal	Arising or situated at the base.
Caudal filaments	Long, segmented, threadlike processes at end of the abdomen; most mayflies have three caudal filaments, a median terminal filament, and two outer cerci (see Fig. 39).
Caudal gills	Three external gills at the tip of the abdomen of Zygoptera (damselflies) (see Fig. 110).
Cephalic fan	The filtering head fans of black fly larvae (see Fig. 92).

Cercus	One of the pair of segmented appendages at the posterior end of the abdomen. Plural: *cerci.*
Cervical	Associated with the neck region, usually the ventral region between the head and prosternum (see Fig. 16).
Concolorous	Similar in color, no distinct differences in color.
Coxa	The basal or first segment of the leg. Plural: *coxae* (see Fig. 16).
Creeping welts	Raised, swollen, or roughened areas often found on dipteran larvae that aide in locomotion (see Figs. 101, 102, 103).
Detritus	Nonliving organic matter.
Diatom	Common name of algae belonging to the phylum Bacillariophyta; often makes up the majority of species within a periphyton community.
Disease vectors	Organisms that usually successfully transmit diseases from animal to animal.
Distal process	A structure located at the tip (see Fig. 61).
Distomedial thumb	A thumblike lobe of the labial palp (see Fig. 53).
Dorsoventrally	From the upper to the lower surface.
Dorsum	Upper surface.
Ecological integrity	Interconnected elements of physical habitat, and the processes that create and maintain them, are capable of supporting and sustaining the full range of biota adapted for that region.
Ecotone	A transition zone.
Emarginate	Notched or indented (see Fig. 44).
Ephemeral	Short-lived, lasting for only a short time.
Eurythermal	A species with broad temperature tolerance.
Eutrophication	Nutrient enrichment leading to greater aquatic production.
Exocuticle	The sclerotized layer of cuticle just outside the endocuticle.

Femur	The leg segment articulated to the trochanter and coxa to the tibia (see Fig. 15).
Fibrils	Threadlike filaments at the base of gill lamellae or plates of mayflies (see Fig. 43a).
Filiform	Hairlike or threadlike antennae.
Forefemora	The femora of the front pair of legs (see Fig. 15).
Foretibia	The tibia of the front pair of legs (see Fig. 15).
Furcal pit	Depressions on the thoracic sternal (especially the mesosternum) sclerites (see Fig. 16).
Fusiform	Tapered torpedo-shaped, fishlike, body form.
Gill(s)	Evagination of the body wall or hindgut that functions in gaseous exchange.
Glossae	One of a pair of lobes on the inner apex of the prementum of the labium (see Fig. 17).
Habitus	The overall appearance.
Hemielytron	The front wings of true bugs or Hemiptera (Heteroptera).
Hemimetabolous	Development where body form and wing development gradually change with each molt. Lacks pupal stage.
Holometabolous	Development where body form abruptly changes during the pupal molt.
Hypopharynx	A sensory structure on the upper surface of the labium.
Hyporheic	Special habitat in sediment interstices beneath the streambed; subsurface habitat.
Hypostome	In larvae of flies, the ventral anterior wedge-shaped sclerite of the head capsule that often bears teeth.
Instars	The growth stage between two successive molts.
Intersegmental setae	Hairs or setae found in the membranous region between segments.
Interstitial	Occurring within the pore spaces between sediment particles.

Intraspecific	Between two or more distinct species.
Labial glands	Usually the "salivary glands" of insects found on the labium.
Labial palpi	A 1–5 segmented appendage of the labium.
Labium	The "lower lip" forming the roof of the preoral cavity and mouth (see Fig. 17).
Lacinia	The mesal lobe of maxillary stipes (see Fig. 17)
Lateral	The side.
Lentic	Referring to calm or slow-moving water habitats such as lakes, reservoirs, ponds, or wetlands.
Ligula	The central portion of the labium or "lower lip" of an insect head.
Lotic	Referring to fast-running water habitats such as rivers and streams.
Macroinvertebrate	Animals that are large enough to be seen by the unaided eye and live at least part of their life cycle within or upon available substrate in a body of water.
Mandibles	The jaws of chewing insects.
Mandibular tusks	"Tusk-like" development of the maxilla (see Fig. 38).
Maxillae	Paired mouthpart structure immediately posterior to the mandibles.
Maxillary palp	A 1–7 segmented sensory appendage born on the maxilla (see Fig. 17).
Mesal	Middle or intermediate.
Mesonotum	The upper surface of the second or middle thoracic segment (see Fig. 15).
Mesosternal	Referring to the underside of the second or middle thoracic segment (see Fig. 16).
Metanotum	The upper surface of the third or last thoracic segment (see Fig. 15).
Molars	The grinding surface of the mandibles.

Morphology	The study of form and structure of organisms.
Multivoltine	A life cycle (egg to adult) producing multiple generations per twelve-month period.
Nearctic	Zoogeographical region comprising North America (the United States, Canada, and Mexico).
Niche	The ecological role of a species in an ecosystem.
Oblique	Slanting, inclined.
Occiput	The dorsal posterior part of the head.
Omnivore	Feeding on a mixed diet of plant and animal material.
Operculate gills	See *operculum*.
Operculum	Hardened first pair of gills that covers the remaining, more delicate gills (see Fig. 39).
Paraglossae	One of a pair of lobes lateral on the prementum of the labium (see Fig. 17).
Paralabial plate	A plate that occurs ventral to the mentum and extends laterally (present in some larvae of the Chironomidae) (see Fig. 106).
Pectinate	Comblike.
Periphyton	Collective term used to describe a community of algae and other microorganisms attached to solid underwater surfaces.
Phylogenetic	Evolutionary lines of descent.
Premandibles	A paired movable feeding appendage that originates from the ventral surface of the labrum (present in some larvae of the Chironomidae) (see Fig. 106).
Prolegs	1. Synonym for pseudopods. 2. Fleshy abdominal legs of certain insect larvae (see Fig. 108).
Pronotal	Referring to the upper surface of the first thoracic segment.
Pronotum	The upper surface of the first thoracic segment (see Fig. 15).

Prostheca	An appendage that arises near the base of the incisors of the mandibles.
Protibia	The tibia of the first pair of legs (see Fig. 15).
Pseudopods	Unjointed (false) legs; see *prolegs*.
Quadrate	Having four sides.
Rectal chamber	The enlarged portion of the rectum of Anisoptera (dragonflies) that bears structures that serve as gills.
Rheotaxis	A behavioral orientation to current (positive rheotaxis = facing upstream).
Sclerites	A hardened body wall plate bounded by sutures or membranous areas.
Sclerotized	Stiffening of the skin, hardened exoskeleton.
Semioperculate	Half or partly covering.
Semivoltine	A life cycle in which a single generation (egg to adult) requires two or more years for completion.
Senescence	Dying back (aquatic plants die back in autumn).
Seston	Organic and inorganic particles suspended in the water column.
Setae	Hairs or hairlike appendages.
Sinuate	To bend in and out.
Spate	A period of high water discharge.
Spinules	Small spines.
Spiracles	External openings of the tracheal system of insects.
Spiracular disc	Disc-shaped structure that bears spiracles (see Fig. 104).
Spring brooks	Streams fed largely by groundwater.
Stenotherm	A species with narrow temperature tolerance. Many mountain stream insects are cold stenotherms.
Sternal	Referring to the ventral surface of the body.
Sternum	A sclerite on the ventral side of the body.
Subapical	Near the tip.

Submental	Pertaining to the submentum, the basal or first sclerite of the labium (see Fig. 17).
Subtriangular	Not completely triangular; angles are not acute.
Suture	An external linelike groove in the body wall.
Tarsal	The leg segment(s) distal to the tibia, comprising 1–5 segments. Plural: *tarsi* (see Fig. 15).
Terga	Referring to the dorsal side of the abdomen.
Tergum	A sclerite on the dorsal side of the abdomen.
Thorax	The middle of the three major divisions of the body of an insect (see Fig. 15).
Tibia	The fourth leg segment, following the femur (see Fig. 15).
Transverse mesosternal ridge	A depression or suture that connects the fork of Y arms on the mesosternum (see Fig. 16).
Trifid	Divided partway to the base into three lobes.
Trochantin	A sclerite in the thoracic wall immediately anterior to the base of the coxa (see Figs. 78, 81, 82, 83).
Tubercles	Wartlike protuberances (see Fig. 40a).
Tusks	Large projections of the mandibles (see Fig. 38).
Univoltine	A life cycle in which a single generation (egg to adult) is produced in a twelve-month period.
Ventral	The undersurface of the body.
Wing pads	The encased undeveloped wings of nymphs of the Hemimetabola (see Fig. 15).

REFERENCES

Alexander, K. D., and K. W. Stewart. 1996. "Description and theoretical considerations of mate finding and other adult behaviors in a Colorado population of *Claassenia sabulosa* (Plecoptera: Perlidae)." *Annals of the American Entomological Society* 82:290–296.

———. 1999. "Revision of the genus *Suwallia* Ricker (Plecoptera: Chloroperlidae)." *Transactions of the American Entomological Society* 125:185–250.

Allan, J. D. 1975. "The distributional ecology and diversity of benthic insects in Cement Creek, Colorado." *Ecology* 56:1040–1053.

———. 1982. "Feeding habits and prey consumption of three setipalpian stoneflies (Plecoptera) in a mountain stream." *Ecology* 63:26–34.

———. 1995. *Stream ecology: Structure and function of running water.* Chapman and Hall, London, England.

Allen, R. K. 1973. "Generic revisions of mayfly nymphs. 1. *Traverella* in North and Central America (Leptophlebiidae)." *Annals of the Entomological Society of America* 66:1287–1295.

———. 1977. "A new species of *Tricorythodes* with notes (Ephemeroptera: Tricorythidae)." *Journal of the Kansas Entomological Society* 50:431–435.

――――. 1980. "Geographical distribution and reclassification of the subfamily Ephemerellidae (Ephemeroptera: Ephemerellidae)," pp. 71–91. In J. F. Flannagan and K. E. Marshall (eds.), *Advances in Ephemeroptera biology*. Plenum, New York.

Allen, R. K., and G. E. Edmunds Jr. 1959. "A revision of the genus *Ephemerella* (Ephemeroptera: Ephemerellidae). I. The subgenus *Timpanoga*." *Canadian Entomologist* 91:51–58.

――――. 1961a. "A revision of the genus *Ephemerella* (Ephemeroptera: Ephemerellidae). II. The subgenus *Caudatella*." *Annals of the Entomological Society of America* 34:161–173.

――――. 1961b. "A revision of the genus *Ephemerella* (Ephemeroptera: Ephemerellidae). III. The subgenus *Attenuatella*." *Journal of the Kansas Entomological Society* 34:161–173.

――――. 1962a. "A revision of the genus *Ephemerella* (Ephemeroptera: Ephemerellidae). IV. The subgenus *Dannella*." *Journal of the Kansas Entomological Society* 35:333–338.

――――. 1962b. "A revision of the genus *Ephemerella* (Ephemeroptera: Ephemerellidae). V. The subgenus *Drunella* in North America." *Miscellaneous Publications of the Entomological Society of America* 3:147–179.

――――. 1963a. "A revision of the genus *Ephemerella* (Ephemeroptera: Ephemerellidae). VI. The subgenus *Serratella* in North America." *Annals of the Entomological Society of America* 56:583–600.

――――. 1963b. "A revision of the genus *Ephemerella* (Ephemeroptera: Ephemerellidae). VII. The subgenus *Eurylophella*." *Canadian Entomologist* 95:597–623.

――――. 1965. "A revision of the genus *Ephemerella* (Ephemeroptera: Ephemerellidae). VII. The subgenus *Ephemerella* in North America." *Miscellaneous Publications of the Entomological Society of America* 4:243–282.

Alstad, D. N. 1980. "Comparative biology of the common Utah Hydropsychidae (Trichoptera)." *American Midland Naturalist* 103:167–174.

Ames, E. L. 1977. "Aquatic insects of two western slope rivers, Colorado." Master of Science thesis, Colorado State University, Fort Collins.

Anderson, N. H., J. R. Sedell, L. M. Roberts, and F. J. Triska. 1978. "The role of aquatic invertebrates in processing of wood debris in coniferous forest streams." *American Midland Naturalist* 100:64–82.

Archangelsky, M. 1997. "Studies on the biology, ecology, and systematics of the immature stages of New World Hydrophiloidea (Coleoptera: Staphyliniformia)." *Bulletin of the Ohio Biological Survey, New Series* 12.

Argyle, D. W., and G. F. Edmunds Jr. 1962. "Mayflies (Ephemeroptera) of the Curecanti Reservoir Basins, Gunnison River, Colorado." *University of Utah Anthropological Papers* 59:179–189.

Armitage, K. B. 1985. "Ecology of the riffle insects of the Firehole River, Wyoming." *Ecology* 39:571–580.

Armitage, P., P. S. Cranston, and L.C.V. Pinder (eds). 1995. *The Chironomidae: The biology and ecology of non-biting midges.* Chapman and Hall, London, England.

Arnett, R. H., Jr., and M. C. Thomas. 2001. *American beetles.* Vol. 1: *Archostemata, Myxophaga, Adephaga, Polyphaga: Staphyliniformia.* CRC Press, Boca Raton, Florida.

Barbour, M. T., J. Gerritsen, G. E. Griffith, R. Frydenborg, E. McCarron, J. S. White, and M. L. Bastin. 1996. "A framework for biological criteria for Florida streams using benthic macroinvertebrates." *Journal of the North American Benthological Society* 15:185–211.

Barbour, M. T., J. Gerritsen, B. D. Snyder, and J. B. Stribling. 1999. "Rapid bioassessment protocols for use in streams and wadable rivers: Periphyton, benthic macroinvertebrates and fish, second edition." EPA 841-B-99-002. U.S. Environmental Protection Agency, Office of Water, Washington, D.C. http://www.epa.gov/OWOW/monitoring/techmon.html.

Baumann, R. W. 1979. "Nearctic stonefly genera as indicators of ecological parameters (Plecoptera: Insecta)." *Great Basin Naturalist* 39:241–244.

Baumann, R. W., A. R. Gaufin, and R. E. Surdick. 1977. "The stoneflies (Plecoptera) of the Rocky Mountains." *Memoirs of the American Entomological Society,* no. 31:1–208.

Beck, W. M., Jr. 1955. "Suggested method for reporting biotic data." *Sewage and Industrial Wastes* 27:1193–1197.

———. 1977. "Environmental requirements and pollution tolerance of common freshwater Chironomidae." EPA-600/4-77-024. United States Environmental Protection Agency, Cincinnati.

Bednarik, A. F., and G. E. Edmunds Jr. 1980. "Descriptions of larval *Heptagenia* from the Rocky Mountain region (Ephemeroptera: Heptageniidae)." *The Pan-Pacific Entomologist* 56:51–62.

Brittain, J. E. 1982. "Biology of mayflies." *Annual Review of Entomology* 27:119–147.

Brown, H. P. 1976. "Aquatic dryopoid beetles (Coleoptera) of the United States." United States Environmental Protection Agency, Cincinnati.

———. 1987. "Biology of riffle beetles." *Annual Review of Entomology* 32:253–373.

Brown, H. P., and D. S. White. 1978. "Notes on separation and identification of North American riffle beetles (Coleoptera: Dryopoidea: Elmidae)." *Entomological News* 89:113.

Brues, C. T. 1927. "Animal life in hot springs." *Quarterly Review of Biology* 2:181–203.

Burian, S. K. 2001. "A revision of the genus *Leptophlebia* Westwood in North America (Ephemeroptera: Leptopohlebiidae: Leptophlebiinae)." *Bulletin of the Ohio Biological Society, New Series* 13, no. 3.

Byers, G. W. 1996. "Tipulidae," pp. 549–570. In R. W. Merritt and K. W. Cummins (eds.), *An introduction to the aquatic insects of North America.* 3rd ed. Kendall/Hunt, Dubuque, Iowa.

Cairns, J., Jr., and J. R. Pratt. 1993. "A history of biological monitoring using macroinvertebrates," pp. 10–27. In D. M. Rosenberg and V. H. Resh (eds.), *Freshwater biomonitoring and benthic macroinvertebrates.* Chapman and Hall, New York.

Canton, S. P., and J. V. Ward. 1981a. "Emergence of Trichoptera from Trout Creek, Colorado, USA." *Series Entomologica* 29:39–45.

———. 1981b. "The aquatic insects, with emphasis on Trichoptera, of a Colorado stream affected by coal strip-mine drainage." *Southwestern Naturalist* 25:453–460.

Cao, Y., and D. P. Larsen. 2001. "Rare species in multivariate analysis for bioassessment: Some considerations." *Journal of the North American Benthological Society* 20:144–153.

Chronic, J., and H. Chronic. 1972. "Prairie, peak and plateau: A guide to the geology of Colorado." *Colorado Geological Survey Bulletin* 32:1–126.

Clements, W. H., D. M. Carlisle, J. M. Lazorchak, and P. C. Johnson. 2000. "Heavy metals structure benthic communities in Colorado mountain streams." *Ecological Applications* 10:626–638.

Clements, W. H., and P. M. Kiffney. 1994. "Integrated laboratory and field approach for assessing impacts of heavy metals at the Arkansas River, Colorado." *Environmental Toxicology and Chemistry* 13:397–404.

Cline, L. D., R. A. Short, and J. V. Ward. 1982. "The influence of highway construction on the macroinvertebrates and epilithic algae of a high mountain stream." *Hydrobiologia* 96:149–159.

Coffman, W. P., and L. C. Ferrington Jr. 1996. "Chironomidae," pp. 635–754. In R. W. Merritt and K. W. Cummins (eds.), *An introduction to the aquatic insects of North America.* 3rd ed. Kendall/Hunt, Dubuque, Iowa.

Collings, M. R. 1969. "Temperature analysis of a stream." United States Geological Survey Professional Paper 650-13:13174–13179.

Colorado Department of Health. 1992. "Colorado Water Quality. Prepared in fulfillment of section 305(b) of the Clean Water Act of 1977." (P.L. 95-217). Water Quality Division.

Contreras-Ramos, A. 1998. *Systematics of the dobsonfly genus* Corydalus (*Megaloptera: Corydalidae*). Thomas Say Publications in Entomology, Entomological Society of America. Monographs.

Corbet, P. S. 1999. *Dragonflies: Behavior and ecology of Odonata*. Comstock Publishing Associates, Ithaca, New York.

Courtney, G. W. 1990. "Revision of Nearctic mountain midges (Diptera: Deuterophlebiidae)." *Journal of Natural History* 24:81–118.

———. 1991. "Life history patterns of Nearctic mountain midges (Diptera: Deuterophlebiidae)." *Journal of the North American Benthological Society* 10:177–197.

Covich, A. P., W. H. Clements, K. D. Fausch, J. D. Stednick, J.Wilkins-Wells, and S. R. Abt. 1995. *Ecological integrity and western water management: A Colorado perspective*. Water in Balance No 3. Colorado Water Resources Research Institute.

Cranston, P. (ed). 1995. *Chironomids from genes to ecosystems*. CSIRO, Victoria, Australia.

Crowson, R. A. 1981. *The biology of the Coleoptera*. Academic Press, London.

Cummins, K. W. 1973. "Trophic relations of aquatic insects." *Annual Review of Entomology* 18:183–206.

———. 1979. "The natural stream ecosystem," pp. 7–24. In J. V. Ward and J. A. Stanford (eds.), *The ecology of regulated streams*. Plenum, New York.

Cummins, K. W., M. A. Wilzbach, D. M. Gates, J. B. Perry, and W. B. Taliaferro. 1989. "Shredders and riparian vegetation." *BioScience* 39:24–30.

Daly, H. V. 1996. "General classification and key to the orders of aquatic and semiaquatic insects," pp. 108–112. In R. W. Merritt and K. W. Cummins (eds.), *An introduction to the aquatic insects of North America*. 3rd ed. Kendall/Hunt, Dubuque, Iowa.

Davies, B. R., and K. F. Walker (eds.). 1986. *The ecology of river systems*. Dr. W. Junk, Dordrecht, Netherlands.

Davis, J. A., and L. A. Barmuta. 1989. "An ecologically useful classification of mean and near-bed flows in streams and rivers." *Freshwater Biology* 21:271–282.

Decamps, H. 1967. "Ecologie des Trichopteres de la vallée d'Aure (Hautes-Pyrénées)." *Annales de Limnologie* 3:399–577.

DeWalt, R. E., and K. W. Stewart. 1995. "Life histories of stoneflies (Plecoptera) in the Rio Conejos of southern Colorado." *The Great Basin Naturalist* 55: 1–18.

DeWalt, R. E., K. W. Stewart, S. R. Moulton II, and J. H. Kennedy. 1994. "Summer emergence of mayflies, stoneflies, and caddisflies from a Colorado mountain stream." *Southwestern Naturalist* 39:249–256.

Dodds, G. S. 1923. "Mayflies from Colorado: Descriptions of certain species and notes on others." *Transactions of the American Entomological Society* 49:93–114.

Dodds, G. S., and E. L. Hisaw. 1924. "Ecological studies of aquatic insects. 1. Adaptations of mayfly nymphs to swift streams." *Ecology* 5:137–148.

———. 1925a. "Ecological studies of aquatic insects. III. Adaptations of caddisfly larvae to swift streams." *Ecology* 6:123–137.

———. 1925b. "Ecological studies of aquatic insects. IV. Altitudinal range and zonation of mayflies, stoneflies and caddisflies in the Colorado Rockies." *Ecology* 6:380–390.

Doughman, I. S. 1983. "A guide to the larvae of the Nearctic Diamesinae (Diptera: Chironomidae). The genera *Boreoheptagyia*, *Protanypus*, *Diamesa*, and *Pseudokiefferiella*." Water Resources Investigations 83-4006. United States Geological Survey.

Durfee, R. S., and B. C. Kondratieff. 1994. "New additions to the inventory of Colorado mayflies (Ephemeroptera)." *Entomological News* 105:222–227.

———. 1999. "Notes on North American *Baetis* (Ephemeroptera: Baetidae): *Baetis moffatti* new synonym of *B. tricaudatus* and range extension for *B. bundyae*." *Entomological News* 110:177–180.

Edmunds, G. F., Jr. 1962. "The principles applied in determining the hierarchic level of the higher categories of Ephemeroptera." *Systematic Zoology* 11:22–31.

Edmunds, G. F., Jr., and R. K. Allen. 1964. "The Rocky Mountain species of *Epeorus* (*Iron*) Eaton (Ephemeroptera: Heptageniidae)." *Journal of the Kansas Entomological Society* 37:275–288.

Edmunds, G. F., Jr., S. L. Jensen, and L. Berner. 1976. *The Mayflies of North and Central America*. University of Minnesota Press, Minneapolis.

Edmunds, G. F., Jr., and W. P. McCafferty. 1984. "*Ephemera compar*: An obscure Colorado burrowing mayfly (Ephemeroptera: Ephemeridae)." *Entomological News* 95:186–188.

Elgmork, K., and O. A. Saether. 1970. "Distribution of invertebrates in a high mountain brook in the Colorado Rocky Mountains." University of Colorado Studies. *Series in Biology* 31:1–55.

Epler, J. H. 1995. "Identification manual for the larval Chironomidae (Diptera) of Florida." Revised edition. Bureau of Surface Water Management, Florida Department of Environmental Protection, Tallahassee, Florida.

Evans, M. A. 1988. "Checklist of the Odonata of Colorado." *Great Basin Naturalist* 48:96–101.

————. 1995. "Checklist of the Odonata of New Mexico with additions to the Colorado checklist." *Proceedings of the Denver Museum of Natural History*. Series 3, no. 8:1–6.

Flint, O. S., Jr. 1984. "The genus *Brachycentrus* in North America, with a proposed phylogeny of the genera of Brachycentridae (Trichoptera)." *Smithsonian Contributions to Zoology*, no. 398.

Floyd, M. A. 1995. "Larvae of the caddisfly genus *Oecetis* (Trichoptera: Leptoceridae) in North America." *Bulletin of Ohio Biological Survey. New Series* 10:1–85.

Frania, H. E., and G. B. Wiggins. 1997. "Analysis of morphological and behavioral evidence for the phylogeny and higher classification of Trichoptera (Insecta)." *Royal Ontario Museum Life Sciences Contributions* 160:1–67.

Fuller, R. L., and K. W. Stewart. 1977. "The food habits of stoneflies (Plecoptera) in the upper Gunnison River, Colorado." *Environmental Entomology* 6:293–302.

————. 1979. "Stonefly (Plecoptera) food habits and prey preference in the Dolores River, Colorado." *Environmental Entomology* 6:293–302.

Gaufin, A. R., and L. Jensen. 1961. "Stoneflies (Plecoptera) from San Juan River in the Navajo Reservoir Basin, Colorado and New Mexico." *University of Utah Anthropological Papers* 55:114–117.

Giller, P. S., and B. Malmqvist. 2000. *The biology of streams and rivers*. Oxford University Press, Oxford.

Givens, D. R., and S. D. Smith. 1980. "A synopsis of the western Arctopsychinae (Trichoptera: Hydropsychidae)." *Melanderia* 35:1–24.

Golterman, H. L. 1975. "Chemistry," pp. 39–80. In B. A. Whitton (ed.), *River Ecology*. Blackwell, Oxford.

Goodnight, C. J. 1973. "The use of aquatic macroinvertebrates as indicators of stream pollution." *Transactions of the American Microscopical Society* 92:1–13.

Gray, L. J., and J. V. Ward. 1979. "Food habits of stream benthos at sites of differing food availability." *American Midland Naturalist* 102:157–167.

―――. 1983. "Leaflitter breakdown in streams receiving treated and untreated metal mine drainage." *Environment International* 9:135–138.

Gray, L. J., J. V. Ward, R. J. Martinson, and E. A. Bergey. 1983. "Aquatic macroinvertebrates of the Piceance Basin, Colorado: Community response along spatial and temporal gradients of environmental conditions." *Southwestern Naturalist* 28:125–135.

Gregory, S. V., F. J. Swanson, W. A. McKee, and K. W. Cummins. 1991. "An ecosystem perspective of riparian zones." *BioScience* 41:540–551.

Haddock, J. D. 1977. "The biosystematics of the caddisfly genus *Nectopsyche* in North America with emphasis on the aquatic stages." *American Midland Naturalist* 98:382–421.

Hagen, K. S. 1996. "Aquatic Hymenoptera," pp. 474–483. In R. W. Merritt and K. W. Cummins (eds.), *An introduction to the aquatic insects of North America*. 3rd ed. Kendall/Hunt, Dubuque, Iowa.

Harper, P. P. 1980. "Phenology and distribution of aquatic dance flies (Diptera: Empididae) in a Laurentian watershed." *American Midland Naturalist* 104:110–177.

Harris, T. L., and T. M. Lawrence. 1978. "Environmental requirements and pollution tolerance of Trichoptera." EPA-600/4-78-063. United States Environmental Protection Agency, Cincinnati.

Haslam, S. M. 1978. *River plants*. Cambridge University Press, Cambridge.

Hawkes, H. A. 1975. "River zonation and classification," pp. 312–374. In B. A. Whitton (ed.), *River ecology*. Blackwell, Oxford.

―――. 1979. "Invertebrates as indicator of river water quality," pp. 2.1–2.45. In A. James and L. Evison (eds.), *Biological indicators of water quality*. Wiley, Chichester, England.

Henry, B. C., Jr. 1993. "A revision of *Neochoroterpes* (Ephemeroptera: Leptophlebiidae) new status." *Transactions of the American Entomological Society* 119:317–333.

Herrmann, S. J., and H. L. Davis. 1991. "Distribution records of *Corydalus cornutus* (Megaloptera: Corydalidae) in Colorado." *Entomological News* 102:25–30.

Herrmann, S. J., D. E. Ruiter, and J. D. Unzicker. 1986. "Distribution and records of Colorado Trichoptera." *Southwestern Naturalist* 31:421–457.

Hogue, C. L. 1987. "Blepharceridae." In G.C.D. Griffiths (ed.), *Flies of the Nearctic Region* 21:1–127.

Hubbard, M. D. 1990. *Mayflies of the world: A catalog of the family and genus group taxa (Insecta: Ephemeroptera)*. Flora and Fauna Handbook No. 8. Sandhill Crane Press, Gainesville, Florida.

Hubbard, M. D., and W. L. Peters. 1978. "Environmental requirements and pollution tolerance of Ephemeroptera." EPA-600/4-78-06 1. United States Environmental Protection Agency, Cincinnati.

Hudson, P. L., D. R. Lenat, B. A. Caldwell, and D. Smith. 1990. "Chironomidae of the southeastern United States: A checklist of species and notes on biology, distribution, and habitat." United States Department of Interior, Fish and Wildlife Service. *Fish and Wildlife Research 7*.

Hutchinson, G. E. 1975. *A treatise on limnology*. Vol. 3. Wiley, New York.

Hynes, H.B.N. 1960. *The biology of polluted waters*. Liverpool University Press, Liverpool, England.

———. 1970a. *The ecology of running waters*. University of Toronto Press, Toronto, Canada.

———. 1970b. "The ecology of stream insects." *Annual Review of Entomology* 15:25–42.

———. 1975. "The stream and its valley." *Internationale Vereinigung für Theoretische und Angewandte Limnologie Verhandlungen* 19:1–15.

———. 1976. "Biology of Plecoptera." *Annual Review of Entomology* 21:135–153.

Illies, J., and L. Botosaneanu. 1963. "Problèmes et méthodes de la classification et de la zonation écologique des eaux courantes, considerées surtout du point de vue faunistique." *Internationale Vereinigung für Theoretische und Angewandte Limnologie Verhandlungen Mitteilungen* 12:1–57.

Jensen, S. L. 1966. "The mayflies of Idaho (Ephemeroptera)." Master of Science thesis, University of Utah, Salt Lake City.

John, P. H. 1978. "Discharge measurement in lower order streams." *Internationale Revue der Gesamten Hydrobiologie* 63:731–755.

Johnson, S. C. 1978. "Larvae of *Ephemerella inermis* and *E. infrequens*." *The Pan-Pacific Entomologist* 54:19–25.

Kamler, E. 1965. "Thermal conditions in mountain waters and their influence on the distribution of Plecoptera and Ephemeroptera larvae." *Ekologia Polska Seria A* 13:377–414.

Karr, J. R., and E. W. Chu. 1999. *Restoring life in running waters: Better biological monitoring*. Island Press, Washington, D.C.

Klemm, D. J., P. A. Lewis, F. Fulk, and J. M. Lazorchak. 1990. "Macroinvertebrate field and laboratory methods for evaluating the biological integrity of surface waters." EPA/600/4-90/030. United States Environmental Protection Agency, Cincinnati.

Knight, A. W. 1963. "Description of the tanyderid larva *Protanyderus margarita* Alexander from Colorado." *Bulletin of the Brooklyn Entomological Society* 58:99–102.

——. 1964. "Description of the tanyderid pupa *Protanyderus margarita* Alexander from Colorado." *Entomological News* 75:237–241.

Knight, A. W., and A. R. Gaufin. 1966. "Altitudinal distribution of stoneflies (Plecoptera) in a Rocky Mountain drainage system." *Journal of the Kansas Entomological Society* 39:668–675.

——. 1967. "Stream type selection and associations of stoneflies (Plecoptera) in a Colorado river drainage system." *Journal of the Kansas Entomological Society* 40:347–352.

Kondratieff, B. C., and R. W. Baumann. 1988. "*Taeniopteryx* of western North America (Plecoptera: Taeniopterygidae)." *The Pan-Pacific Entomologist* 64:381–390.

——. In press. "A review of the stoneflies (Plecoptera) of Colorado, U.S.A." *Western North American Naturalist*.

Kondratieff, B. C., and J. R. Voshell Jr. 1984. "The North and Central American species of *Isonychia* (Ephemeroptera: Oligoneuriidae)." *Transactions of the American Entomological Society* 110:129–244.

Kondratieff, B. C., and J. V. Ward. 1987. "*Taeniopteryx burksi* (Plecoptera: Taeniopterygidae) in Colorado, with notes on aquatic insects of Plains streams." *Entomological News* 98:13–16.

Koss, R. W., and G. F. Edmunds Jr. 1970. "A new species of *Lachlania* from New Mexico with notes on the genus (Ephemeroptera: Oligoneuriidae)." *Proceedings of the Entomological Society of Washington* 72:55–65.

Lamberti, G. A., and V. H. Resh. 1983. "Geothermal effects on stream benthos: Separate influences of thermal and chemical components on periphyton and macroinvertebrates." *Canadian Journal of Fisheries and Aquatic Sciences* 40:1995–2009.

Landa, V. 1968. "Developmental cycles of central European Ephemeroptera and their interrelations." *Acta Entomologica Bohemoslovaca* 65:276–284.

Larson, D. J., Y. Alarie, and R. E. Roughley. 2000. *Predaceous diving beetles (Coleoptera: Dytiscidae) of the Nearctic region, with emphasis on the fauna of Canada and Alaska.* National Research Council, NCR Research Press, Ottawa.

Lenat, D. R. 1993. "A biotic index for the southeastern United States: Derivation and list of tolerance values, with criteria for assigning water-quality ratings." *Journal of the North American Benthological Society* 12:279–290.

Leopold, L. B. 1997. *Water, rivers and creeks.* University Science Books, Sausalito, California.

Leopold, L. B., M. G. Wolman, and J. P. Miller. 1964. *Fluvial processes in geomorphology.* Freeman, San Francisco.

LeSage, L., and P. P. Harper. 1976. "Cycles biologiques d'Elmidae (Coleopteres) de ruisseaux des Laurentides, Quebec." *Annals de Limnologie* 12:139–174.

Lloyd, M., and R. J. Ghelardi. 1964. "A table for calculating the 'equitability' component of species diversity." *Journal of Animal Ecology* 33:217–225.

Lock, M. A., R. R. Wallace, J. W. Costerton, R. M. Ventullo, and S. E. Chariton. 1984. "River epilithon: Toward a structural-functional model." *Oikos* 42:10–22.

Lugo-Ortiz, C. R., and W. P. McCafferty. 1998. "A new North American genus of Baetidae (Ephemeroptera) and key to *Baetis* complex genera." *Entomological News* 109:345–353.

Lugo-Ortiz, C. R., W. P. McCafferty, and R. D. Waltz. 1999. "Definition and reorganization of the genus *Pseudocloeon* (Ephemeroptera: Baetidae) with new species descriptions and combinations." *Transactions of the American Entomological Society* 125:1–37.

Macan, T. T. 1961. "Factors that limit the range of freshwater animals." Biological Reviews. *Cambridge Philosophical Society* 36:151–198.

———. 1974. "Running water." *Internationale Vereinigung für Theoretische und Angewandte Limnologie Verhandlungen Mitteilungen* 20:301–321.

MacDonald, J. F., and J. R. Harkridger. 1999. "Differentiation of larvae of *Metachela* Coquillett and *Neoplasta* Coquillett (Diptera: Empididae: Hemerodromiinae) based on larval rearing, external morphology, and ribosomal DNA fragment size." *Journal of the North American Benthological Society* 18:414–419.

Malanson, G. P. 1993. *Riparian landscapes.* Cambridge University Press, Cambridge.

Martinson, R. J., and J. V Ward. 1982. "Life history and ecology of *Hesperophylax occidentalis* (Banks) (Trichoptera: Limnephilidae) from three springs in the Piceance Basin, Colorado." *Freshwater Invertebrate Biology* 1:41–47.

Mason, W. T., Jr. 1973. "An introduction to the identification of chironomid larvae." United States Environmental Protection Agency, Cincinnati.

McAlpine, J. E., B. V. Peterson, G. E. Shewell, H. J. Teskey, J. R. Vockeroth, and D. M. Wood (eds.). 1981. *Manual of Nearctic Diptera.* Vol. 1. Monograph no. 27. Research Branch, Agriculture Canada, Ottawa, Ontario.

————. 1987. *Manual of Nearctic Diptera.* Vol. 2. Monograph no. 28. Research Branch, Agriculture Canada, Ottawa, Ontario.

McCafferty, W. P. 1975. "The burrowing mayflies (Ephemeroptera: Ephemeroidea) of the United States." *Transactions of the American Entomological Society* 101:447–504.

————. 1991. "Toward a phylogenetic classification of the Ephemeroptera (Insecta): A commentary on systematics." *Annals of the Entomological Society of America* 84:343–360.

————. 1994. "Distributional and classificatory supplement to the burrowing mayflies (Ephemeroptera: Ephemeroidea) of the United States." *Entomological News* 105:1–13.

————. 1996. "The Ephemeroptera species of North America and index to their complete nomenclature." *Transactions of the American Entomological Society* 122:1–54.

————. 1997. "Ephemeroptera," pp. 89–117. In R. W. Poole and P. Gentili (eds), *Nomina Insecta Nearctica, a checklist of the insects of North America.* Vol. 4: *Non-holometabolous orders.* Entomological Information Services, Rockville, Maryland.

McCafferty, W. P., R. S. Durfee, and B. C. Kondratieff. 1993. "Colorado mayflies (Ephemeroptera): An annotated inventory." *The Southwestern Naturalist* 38:252–274.

McCafferty, W. P., and G. F. Edmunds Jr. 1979. "The higher classification of the Ephemeroptera, and its evolutionary basis." *Annals of the Entomological Society of America* 72:5–12.

McCafferty, W. P., and R. P. Randolph. 2000. "Further contributions to the spatulate clawed Baetidae (Ephemeroptera)." *Entomological News* 111:259–264.

McCafferty, W. P., and R. D. Waltz. 1990. "Revisionary synopsis of the Baetidae (Ephemeroptera) of North and Middle America." *Transactions of the American Entomological Society* 116:769–799.

————. 1995. "*Labiobaetis* (Ephemeroptera: Baetidae): New status, new North American species, and related new genus." *Entomological News* 106:19–28.

McCafferty, W. P., and T. Q. Wang. 2000. "Phylogenetic systematics of the major lineages of pannot mayflies (Ephemeroptera: Pannota)." *Transactions of the American Entomological Society* 126:9–101.

McCafferty, W. P., M. J. Wigle, and R. D. Waltz. 1994. "Systematics and biology of *Acentrella turbida* (McDunnough) (Ephemeroptera: Baetidae)." *Pan-Pacific Entomologist* 70:301–308.

McFadden, M. W. 1967. "Soldier fly larvae in America north of Mexico." *Proceedings of United States National Museum* 121:1–72.

McKnight, D. M., and G. Feder. 1984. "The ecological effect of acid conditions and precipitation of hydrous metal oxides in a Rocky Mountain stream." *Hydrobiologia* 119:129–138.

Mecom, J. O. 1972a. "Productivity and distribution of Trichoptera larvae in a Colorado mountain stream." *Hydrobiologia* 40:151–176.

———. 1972b. "Feeding habits of Trichoptera in a mountain stream." *Oikos* 23:401–407.

Merritt, R. W., and K. W. Cummins (eds.). 1996. *An introduction to the aquatic insects of North America*. 3rd ed. Kendall/Hunt, Dubuque, Iowa.

Minshall, G. W. 1978. "Autotrophy in stream ecosystems." *BioScience* 28:767–771.

———. 1984. "Aquatic insect, substratum relationships," pp. 358–400. In V. H. Resh and D. M. Rosenberg (eds.), *The ecology of aquatic insects*. Praeger, New York.

Morihara, D. K., and W. P. McCafferty. 1979. "The *Baetis* larvae of North America (Ephemeroptera: Baetidae)." *Transactions of the American Entomological Society* 105:139–221.

Morse, J. C. 1993. "A checklist of the Trichoptera of North America, including Greenland and Mexico." *Transactions of the America Entomological Society* 119:47–93.

———. 1997. "Phylogeny of Trichoptera." *Annual Review of Entomology* 42:427–450.

Morse, J. C., and R. W. Holzental. 1996. "Trichoptera genera," pp. 350–386. In R. W. Merrit and K. W. Cummins (eds.), *An introduction to the aquatic insects of North America*. 3rd ed. Kendall/Hunt, Dubuque, Iowa.

Müller, K. 1982. "The colonization cycle of freshwater insects." *Oecologia* 52:202–207.

Naiman, R. J., and H. Decamps. 1997. "The ecology of interfaces: Riparian zones." *Annual Review of Ecology and Systematics* 28:621–658.

Needham, P. R., and R. L. Usinger. 1956. "Variability in the macrofauna of a single riffle in Prosser Creek, California, as indicated by the Surber sampler." *Hilgardia* 24:383–409.

Needham, J. G., M. J. Westfall Jr., and M. May. 2000. *Dragonflies of North America*. Scientific Publishers, Gainesville, Florida.

Nelson, C. R., and R. W. Baumann. 1987. "The winter stonefly genus *Capnura* (Plecoptera: Capniidae) in North America: Systematics, phylogeny, and zoogeography." *Transactions of the American Entomological Society* 113:1–28.

——. 1989. "Systematics and distribution of the winter stonefly genus *Capnia* (Plecoptera: Capniidae) in North America." *The Great Basin Naturalist* 49:289–363.

Norris, R. H., and A. Georges. 1993. "Analysis and interpretation of benthic macroinvertebrate surveys," pp. 234–286. In D. M. Rosenberg and V. H. Resh (eds.), *Freshwater biomonitoring and benthic macroinvertebrates*. Chapman and Hall, New York.

Nowell, W. R. 1951. "The dipterous family Dixidae in western North America (Insecta: Diptera)." *Microentomology* 16:187–270.

Oliver, D. R., and M. E. Roussel. 1983. *The insects and arachnids of Canada. Part 2: The genera of larval midges of Canada. Diptera: Chironomidae*. Publication 1746. Agriculture Canada, Ottawa, Ontario.

Parker, C. R., and G. B. Wiggins. 1985. "The Nearctic caddisfly genus *Hesperophylax* (Trichoptera: Limnephilidae)." *Canadian Journal of Zoology* 61:2443–2472.

Pearl, R. H. 1972. "Geothermal resources of Colorado." *Colorado Geological Survey, Special Publications* 2:1–54.

Peck, D. L., and S. D. Smith. 1978. "A revision of the *Rhyacophila coloradensis* complex (Trichoptera: Rhyacophilidae)." *Melanderia* 27:1–24.

Peckarsky, B. L. 1980. "Predator-prey interactions between stoneflies and mayflies: Behavioral observations." *Ecology* 61:932–943.

Peckarsky, B. L., and K. Z. Cook. 1981. "Effects of Keystone Mine effluent on colonization of stream benthos." *Environmental Entomology* 10:864–871.

Peckarsky, B. L., S. L. Dodson, and D. J. Conklin Jr. 1985. "A key to the aquatic insects of streams in the vicinity of the Rocky Mountain Biological Lab, including chironomid larvae from streams and ponds." Colorado Division of Wildlife, Denver.

Pennak, R. W. 1977. "Trophic variables in Rocky Mountain trout streams." *Archiv für Hydrobiologie* 80:253–285.

——. 1978. *Fresh-water invertebrates of the United States*. Wiley, New York.

Pescador, M. L., and W. L. Peters. 1980. "A revision of the genus *Homoeoneuria* (Ephemeroptera: Oligoneuriidae)." *Transactions of the American Entomological Society* 106:357–393.

Peters, T. M., and E. F. Cook. 1966. "The Nearctic Dixidae (Diptera)." *Miscellaneous Publications of the Entomological Society of America* 5:233–278.

Peters, W. L., and G. F. Edmunds Jr. 1961. "The mayflies (Ephemeroptera) of the Navajo Reservoir Basin, New Mexico and Colorado." *University of Utah Anthropological Papers* 55:107–111.

Peterson, B. V., and B. C. Kondratieff. 1994. "The blackflies (Diptera: Simuliidae) of Colorado: An annotated list with keys, illustrations and descriptions of three species." *Memoirs of the American Entomological Society*, no. 42:1–121.

Petts, G. E. 1984. *Impounded rivers*. Wiley, Chichester, England.

Plafkin, J. L., M. T. Barbour, K. D. Porter, S. K. Gross, and R. M. Hughes. 1989. "Rapid bioassessment protocols for use in streams and rivers: Benthic macroinvertebrates and fish." EPA 440-4-89-001. U.S. Environmental Protection Agency, Office of Water Regulations and Standards, Washington, D.C.

Platts, W. S., W. F. Megahan, and G. W. Minshall. 1983. *Methods for evaluating stream, riparian, and biotic conditions*. United States Department of Agriculture, Forest Service. Intermountain Forest and Range Experiment Station, Ogden, Utah.

Poff, N. L., and J. V. Ward. 1989. "Implications of stream flow variability and predictability for lotic community structure: A regional analysis of stream flow patterns." *Canadian Journal of Fisheries and Aquatic Sciences* 46:1805–1818.

Pritchard, G. 1983. "Biology of Tipulidae." *Annual Review of Entomology* 28:1–22.

Provonsha, A. V. 1990. "A revision of the genus *Caenis* in North America (Ephemeroptera: Caenidae)." *Transactions of the American Entomological Society* 116:801–884.

Rader, R. B., and J. V. Ward. 1987a. "Resource utilization, overlap and temporal dynamics in a guild of mountain stream insects." *Freshwater Biology* 18:521–528.

———. 1987b. "Mayfly production in a Colorado mountain stream: An assessment of methods for synchronous and non-synchronous species." *Hydrobiologia* 148:145–150.

———. 1989. "Influence of impoundments on mayfly diets, life histories, and production." *Journal of the North American Benthological Society* 8:64–73.

Resh, V. H., and D. M. Rosenberg (eds.). 1984. *The ecology of aquatic insects*. Praeger, New York.

Reynoldson, T. B., R. C. Bailey, K. E. Day, and R. H. Norris. 1995. "Biological guidelines for freshwater sediment based on BEnthic Assessment of

SedimenT (the BEAST) using a multivariate approach for predicting biological state." *Australian Journal of Ecology* 20:198–219.

Reynoldson, T. B., R. H. Norris, V. H. Resh, K. E. Day, and D. M. Rosenberg. 1997. "The reference condition: A comparison of multimetric and multivariate approaches to assess water quality impairment using benthic communities." *Journal of the North American Benthological Society* 16:833–852.

Richardson, T. W., and A. R. Gaufin. 1971. "Food habits of some western stonefly nymphs." *Transactions of the American Entomological Society* 97:91–121.

Rosenberg D. M., and V. H. Resh. 1993. "Introduction to freshwater biomonitoring and benthic macroinvertebrates," pp. 1–9. In D. M. Rosenberg and V. H. Resh (eds.), *Freshwater biomonitoring and benthic macroinvertebrates*. Chapman and Hall, New York.

Ross, H. H. 1956. "Evolution and classification of the mountain caddisflies." University of Illinois Press, Urbana.

Ruiter, D. E. 1990. "A new species of *Neotrichia* (Trichoptera: Hydroptilidae) from Colorado with additions and corrections to the distribution and records of Colorado Trichoptera." *Entomological News* 10:88–92.

———. 1995. "The adult *Limnephilus* leach (Trichoptera: Limnephilidae) of the New World." *Bulletin of the Ohio Biological Survey, New Series* 11:1–200.

———. 1999. "A new species and new synonym in the genus *Psychornia* (Limnephilidae), with significant records for caddisflies (Trichoptera) from western North America." *The Great Basin Naturalist* 59:160–168.

———. 2000. "Generic key to the adult ocellate Limnephiloidea of the Western Hemisphere (Insecta: Trichoptera)." *Ohio Biological Survey Miscellaneous Contributions* no. 5.

Ruse, L. R., and S. J. Herrmann. 2000. "Plecoptera and Trichoptera species distribution related to environmental characteristics of the metal-polluted Arkansas River, Colorado." *Western North American Naturalist* 60:57–65.

Ruse, L. R., S. J. Herrmann, and J. E. Sublette. 2000. "Chironomidae (Diptera) species distribution related to environmental characteristics of the metal-polluted Arkansas River, Colorado." *Western North American Naturalist* 60:34–56.

Ruttner, F. 1926. "Bermerkungen über den Sauerstoffgehalt der Gewasser und dessen respiratorischen." *Wertpapier Naturwissenschaften* 14:1237–1239.

Saether, O. A. 1970. "Chironomids and other invertebrates from North Boulder Creek, Colorado." *University of Colorado Studies, Series in Biology* 31:59–114.

Sandberg, J. B., and K. W. Stewart. 2001. "Drumming behavior and life history notes of a high-altitude Colorado population of the stonefly *Isoperla petersoni:* Needham & Christenson (Plecoptera: Perlodidae)." *Western North American Naturalist* 61:445–451.

Schefter, P. W., and G. B. Wiggins. 1986. *A systematic study of the Nearctic larvae of the Hydropsyche morosa group (Trichoptera: Hydropsychidae).* Miscellaneous Publications. Royal Ontario Museum Life Sciences, Toronto.

Schmude, K. L., and H. P. Brown. 1991. "A new species of *Stenelmis* (Coleoptera: Elmidae) found west of the Mississippi River." *Proceedings of the Entomological Society of Washington* 93:51–61.

Seagle, H. J., Jr. 1982. "Comparison of the food habits of three species of riffle beetles, *Stenelmis crenata*, *Stenelmis mera*, and *Optioservus trivittatus* (Coleoptera: Dryopoidea: Elmidae)." *Freshwater Invertebrate Biology* 1:33–38.

Shannon, C. E., and W. Weaver. 1963. *The mathematical theory of communication.* University of Illinois Press, Urbana.

Short, R. A., S. P. Canton, and J. V. Ward. 1980. "Detrital processing and associated macroinvertebrates in a Colorado mountain stream." *Ecology* 61:727–732.

Short, R. A., and J. V. Ward. 1980a. "Macroinvertebrates of a Colorado high mountain stream." *Southwestern Naturalist* 25:23–32.

———. 1980b. "Leaf litter processing in a regulated Rocky Mountain stream." *Canadian Journal of Fisheries and Aquatic Sciences* 37:123–127.

———. 1980c. "Life history and production of *Skwala parallela* (Frison) (Plecoptera: Perlodidae) in a montane stream." *Hydrobiologia* 69:273–275.

———. 1981. "Trophic ecology of three winter stoneflies (Plecoptera)." *American Midland Naturalist* 105:341–347.

Shoutis, A. H. 1981. "Distribution of the Chironomidae in the upper Poudre River." Master of Science thesis, Colorado State University, Fort Collins.

Simpson, J., R. Norris, L. Barmuta, and P. Blackman. 1996. "Australian river assessment system: National River Health Program predictive model manual." <http.//ausrivas.Canberra.au>.

Simpson, K. W., and R. W. Bem. 1980. "Common larvae of Chironomidae (Diptera) from New York state streams and rivers." *New York State Museum Bulletin,* no. 439:1–105.

Simpson, K. W., and R. W. Bode. 1980. "Common larvae of Chironomdae (Diptera) from New York State streams and rivers." *New York State Museum Bulletin* 439:1–105.

Smith, K. 1972. "River water temperatures: An environmental review." *Scottish Geographical Magazine* 88:211–220.

Smith, K., and M. E. Lavis. 1975. "Environmental influence on the temperature of a small upland stream." *Oikos* 26:228–236.

Smith, S. D. 1968. "The *Rhyacophila* of the Salmon River drainage of Idaho with special reference to larvae." *Annals of the Entomological Society of America* 61:655–674.

Soldan, T. 1986. "A revision of Caenidae with ocellar tubercles in the nymphal stage (Ephemeroptera)." *Acta Universitatis Carolinae-Biologica 1982– 1984:289–362.*

Sparks, T. H., W. A. Scott, and R. T. Clarke. 1999. "Traditional multivariate techniques: Potential for use in ecotoxicology." *Environmental Toxicology and Chemistry* 18:128–137.

Stanger, J. A., and R. W. Baumann. 1993. "A revision of the stonefly genus *Taenionema* (Plecoptera: Taeniopterygidae)." *Transactions of the American Entomological Society* 119:171–229.

Stanford, J. A., and J. V. Ward. 1981. "Preliminary interpretations of the distribution of Hydropsychidae in a regulated river." *Series Entomologica* 20:323–328.

———. 1988. "The hyporheic habitat of river ecosystems." *Nature* 335:64–66.

Stark, B. P., and J. W. Kyzar. 2000. "Systematics of Nearctic *Paraleuctra* with description of a new genus (Plecoptera: Leuctridae)." *Tijdschrift voor Entomologie* 144:119–135.

Stark, B. P., S. W. Szczytko, and R. W. Baumann. 1986. "North American stoneflies (Plecoptera): Systematics, distribution, and taxonomic references." *The Great Basin Naturalist* 46:383–397.

Stark, B. P., S. W. Szczytko, and C. R. Nelson. 1998. *American stoneflies: A photographic guide to the Plecoptera.* Caddis Press, Columbus, Ohio.

Statzner, B., and T. E. Holme. 1989. "Morphological adaptation of shape to flow: Microcurrents around lotic macroinvertebrates with known Reynolds numbers at quasi-natural flow conditions." *Oecologia* 78:145–157.

Stewart, K. W., and B. P. Stark. 1988. *Nymphs of North American stonefly genera (Plecoptera).* Thomas Say Foundation. Entomological Society of America, no. 12.

Steyskal, G. C., and L. V. Knutson. 1981. "Empididae," pp. 607–624. In McAlpine et al. (eds.), *Manual of Nearctic Diptera*. Vol. 1. Monograph no. 27. Research Branch, Agriculture Canada, Ottawa, Ontario.

Strahler, A. N. 1957. "Quantitative analysis of watershed geomorphology." *Transactions, American Geophysical Union* 38:913–920.

Stribling, J. B., B. K. Jessup, J. Gerritsen. 2000. *Development of biological and physical habitat criteria for Wyoming streams and their use in the TMDL process*. Report to U.S. EPA Region 8, Denver, Colorado.

Surdick, R. F. 1985. *Nearctic genera of Chloroperlinae (Plecoptera: Chloroperlidae)*. Illinois Biological Monographs 54. University of Illinois Press, Champaign.

Surdick, R. F., and A. R. Gaufin. 1978. *Environmental requirements and pollution tolerance of Plecoptera*. EPA-600/4-78-062. United States Environmental Protection Agency, Cincinnati.

Szczytko, S. W., and K. W. Stewart. 1979. "The genus *Isoperla* (Plecoptera) of western North America: Holomorphology and systematics, and a new stonefly genus *Cascadoperla*." *Memoirs of the American Entomological Society*, no. 32:1–120.

Taylor, B. W., C. R. Anderson, and P. L. Peckarsky. 1999. "Delayed egg hatching and semivoltinism in the Nearctic stonefly *Megarcys signata* (Plecoptera: Perlodidae)." *Aquatic Insects* 21:179–185.

Thut, R. N. 1969. "Feeding habits of larvae of seven *Rhyacophila* (Trichoptera: Rhyacophilidae) species with notes on other life-history features." *Annals of the Entomological Society of America* 62:894–898.

Townsend, G. D., and G. Pritchard. 2000. "Egg development in the stonefly *Pteronarcys californica* Newport (Plecoptera: Pteronarcyidae)." *Aquatic Insects* 22:19–26.

United States Department of Agriculture Forest Service. 1989. "Aquatic ecosystem inventory: Macroinvertebrate inventory." Chapter 5 in *Fisheries habitat survey handbook* (R-4 FSH 2609.23). Intermountain Region.

Usinger, R. L. 1956. "Aquatic Hemiptera," pp. 182–228. In R. L. Usinger (ed.), *Aquatic insects of California*. University of California Press, Berkeley.

Vannote, R. L., G. W. Minshall, K. W. Cummins, J. R. Sedell, and C. E. Cushing. 1980. "The river continuum concept." *Canadian Journal of Fisheries and Aquatic Sciences* 37:130–137.

Vineyard, R. N., and G. B. Wiggins. 1988. "Further revision of the caddisfly family Uenoidae (Trichoptera): Evidence for inclusion of Neophylacinae and Thremmatidae." *Systematic Entomology* 13:361–372.

Vineyard, R. N., G. B. Wiggins, H. E. Frania, and P. W. Schefter. In press. "Systematics of the caddisfly genus *Neophylax*." *Royal Ontario Museum Life Sciences Contributions.*

Voshell, J. R., Jr. 2001. *A guide to common freshwater invertebrates of North America.* University of Nebraska Press, Lincoln.

Wallace, J. B., and R. W. Merritt. 1980. "Filter-feeding ecology of aquatic insects." *Annual Review of Entomology* 25:103–132.

Walshe, B. M. 1950. "The function of haemoglobin in *Chironomus plumosus* under natural conditions." *Journal of Experimental Biology* 27:73–95.

Waltz, R. D., and W. P. McCafferty. 1979. "Freshwater springtails (Hexapoda: Collembola) of North America." Purdue University. Agriculture Experiment Station Research Bulletin 960.

———. 1987a. "New genera of Baetidae for some Nearctic species previously included in *Baetis* Leach (Ephemeroptera)." *Annals of the Entomological Society of America* 80:667–670.

———. 1987b. "Systematics of *Pseudocloeon, Acentrella, Baetiella,* and *Liebebiella,* new genus (Ephemeroptera: Baetidae)." *Journal of the New York Entomological Society* 95:553–568.

Ward, J. V. 1975. "Bottom fauna-substrate relationships in a northern Colorado trout stream: 1945 and 1974." *Ecology* 56:1424–1429.

———. 1976a. "Effects of thermal constancy and seasonal temperature displacement on community structure of stream macroinvertebrates," pp. 302–307. In G. W. Esch and R. W. McFarlane (eds.), *Thermal ecology II.* ERDA Symposium Series, Augusta, Georgia.

———. 1976b. "Effects of flow patterns below large dams on stream benthos: A review," pp. 235–253. In J. F. Orsborn and C. H. Allman (eds.), *Instream flow needs.* Vol. 2. American Fisheries Society, Washington, D.C.

———. 1981. "Altitudinal distribution and abundance of Trichoptera in a Rocky Mountain stream." *Series Entomologica* 20:375–381.

———. 1982. "Altitudinal zonation of Plecoptera, in a Rocky Mountain stream." *Aquatic Insects* 4:105–110.

———. 1984a. "Diversity patterns exhibited by the Plecoptera of a Colorado mountain stream." *Annales de Limnologie* 20:123–128.

———. 1984b. "Ecological perspectives in the management of aquatic insect habitat," pp. 558–577. In V. H. Resh and D. M. Rosenberg (eds.), *The ecology of aquatic insects.* Praeger, New York.

———. 1985. "Thermal characteristics of running waters." *Hydrobiologia* 125:31–46.

————. 1986. "Altitudinal zonation in a Rocky Mountain stream." *Archiv für Hydrobiologie* 74:133–199.

————. 1987. "Trichoptera of regulated Rocky Mountain streams." *Series Entomologica* 39:375–380.

————. 1992a. *Aquatic insect ecology.* Vol. 1: *Biology and habitat.* Wiley, New York.

————. 1992b. "A mountain river," pp. 493–510. In P. Calow and G. L. Petts (eds.), *Rivers handbook: Hydrological and ecological principles.* Blackwell, Oxford.

Ward, J. V., and L. Berner. 1980. "Abundance and altitudinal distribution of Ephemeroptera in a Rocky Mountain stream," pp. 169–178. In J. E. Flannagan and K. E. Marshall (eds.), *Advances in Ephemeroptera biology.* Plenum, New York.

Ward, J. V., S. P. Canton, and L. J. Gray. 1978. "The stream environment and macroinvertebrate communities: Contrasting effects of mining in Colorado and the eastern United States," pp. 176–187. In J. H. Thorp and J. W. Gibbons (eds.), *Energy and environmental stress in aquatic systems.* DOE Symposium Series, Springfield, Virginia.

Ward, J. V., and R. G. Dufford. 1979. "Longitudinal and seasonal distribution of macroinvertebrates and epilithic algae in a Colorado spring brook-pond system." *Archiv für Hydrobiologie* 86:284–321.

Ward, J. V., and D. Garcia de Jalon. 1991. "Ephemeroptera of regulated mountain streams in Spain and Colorado." In J. Alba-Tercedor and A. Sanchez-Ortega (eds.), *Overview and strategies of Ephemeroptera and Plecoptera.* Sandhill Crane Press, Gainesville, Florida.

Ward, J. V., and R. A. Short. 1978. "Macroinvertebrate community structure of four special lotic habitats in Colorado, U.S.A." *Internationale Vereinigung für Theoretische und Angewandte Limnologie Verhandlungen* 20:1382–1387.

Ward, J. V., and J. A. Stanford (eds.). 1979. *The ecology of regulated streams.* Plenum, New York.

————. 1982. "Thermal responses in the evolutionary ecology of aquatic insects." *Annual Review of Entomology* 27:97–117.

————. 1990. "Ephemeroptera of the Gunnison River, Colorado, U.S.A.," pp. 215–220. In I. Campbell (ed.), *Mayflies and stoneflies: Life histories and biology.* Kluwer, Dordrecht, Netherlands.

Ward, J. V., H. J. Zimmermann, and L. D. Cline. 1986. "Lotic zoobenthos of the Colorado River system." In B. R. Davies and K. E. Walker (eds.), *Ecology of river systems.* Monographiae Biologicae, Dr. W. Junk, The Hague.

Waters, T. F. 1995. *Sediment in streams: Sources, biological effects, and control.* American Fisheries Society Monograph 7.

———. 2000. *Wildstream: A natural history of the free-flowing river.* Riparian Press, St. Paul, Minnesota.

Weaver, J. S., III. 1988. "A synopsis of the North American Lepidostomatidae (Trichoptera)." *Contributions of the North American Entomological Institute* 24:1–141.

Webb, D. W. 1977. "The Nearctic Athericidae (Insecta: Diptera)." *Journal of the Kansas Entomological Society* 50:473–495.

Weber, C. I. 1973. "Biological field and laboratory methods for measuring the quality of surface waters and effluents." EPA-670/4-73-001. United States Environmental Protection Agency, Cincinnati.

Wentz, D. A. 1974. "Effect of mine drainage on the quality of streams in Colorado, 1971–72." Colorado Water Resources Circular no. 21, Colorado Water Conservation Board, Denver.

Westfall, M. J., Jr., and M. L. May. 1996. *Damselflies of North America.* Scientific Publishers, Gainesville, Florida.

Westlake, D. E. 1975. "Macrophytes," pp. 106–128. In B. A. Whitton (ed.), *River ecology.* Blackwell, Oxford.

Wetzel, R. G. 1983. *Limnology.* 2nd ed. W. B. Saunders, Philadelphia.

White, D. S. 1978. "A revision of the Nearctic *Optioservus* (Coleoptera: Elmidae), with descriptions of new species." *Systematic Entomology* 3:59–74.

Whitton, B. A. (ed.). 1975. *River ecology.* Blackwell, Oxford.

Wiederholm, T. 1984. "Responses of aquatic insects to environmental pollution," pp. 508–557. In V. H. Resh and D. M. Rosenberg (eds.), *The ecology of aquatic insects.* Praeger, New York.

———. 1986. *Chironomidae of the Holarctic region: Keys and diagnoses.* Part 2: *Pupae.* Entomologica Scandinavica, supplement no. 28.

Wiederholm, T. (ed.). 1983. *Chironomidae of the Holarctic region: Keys and diagnoses.* Part 1: *Larvae.* Entomologica Scandinavica, supplement no. 19.

Wiersema, N. A., and W. P. McCafferty. 2000. "Generic revision of the North and Central American Leptohyphidae (Ephemeroptera: Pannota)." *Transactions of the American Entomological Society* 126:337–371.

Wiggins, G. B. 1996. *Larvae of the North American caddisfly genera (Trichoptera).* 2nd ed. University of Toronto Press, Toronto, Ontario.

Wiggins, G. B., and R. J. Mackay. 1978. "Some relationships between systematics and trophic ecology in Nearctic aquatic insects, with special reference to Trichoptera." *Ecology* 59:1211–1220.

Wiggins, G. B., J. S. Weaver III, and J. D. Unzicker. 1985. "Revision of the caddisfly family Uenoidae (Trichoptera)." *Canadian Entomologist* 117:763–800.

Wiggins, G. B., and W. Wichard. 1989. "Phylogeny of pupation in Trichoptera, with proposals on the origin and higher classification of the order." *Journal of the North American Benthological Society* 8:260–276.

Wilhm, J. L. 1970. "Range of diversity index in benthic macroinvertebrate populations." *Journal of the Water Pollution Control Federation* 42:R221-11224.

———. 1975. "Biological indicators of pollution," pp. 376–402. In B. A. Whitton (ed.), *River ecology*. Blackwell, Oxford.

Wilhm, J. L., and T. C. Dorris. 1968. "Biological parameters of water quality." *BioScience* 18:477–481.

Williams, D. D. 1987. *The ecology of temporary waters*. Timber Press, Portland, Oregon.

Williams, D. D., and B. W. Feltmate. 1992. *Aquatic insects*. CAB International, Wallingford, England.

Williams, D. D., A. F. Tavares, and E. Bryant. 1987. "Respiratory device or camouflage?—A case for the caddisfly." *Okios* 50:42–52.

Winterbourn, M. J. 1968. "The faunas of thermal waters in New Zealand." *Tuatara* 16:111–122.

Wohl, E. E. 2000. *Mountain rivers*. Water Resources Mongraph 14. American Geophysical Union, Washington, D.C.

———. 2001. *Virtual rivers: Lessons from the mountain rivers of the Colorado Front Range*. Yale University Press, New Haven, Connecticut.

Wohl, E. E., and D. A. Cenderelli. 2000. "Sediment and transport patterns following a reservoir sediment release." *Water Resources Research* 36:319–334.

Wold, J. L. 1973. "Systematics of the genus *Rhyacophila* (Trichoptera: Rhyacophilidae) in North America with special reference to the immature stages." Master of Science thesis, Oregon State University, Corvallis.

Yang, C. T. 1971. "Formation of riffles and pools." *Water Research* 7:1567–1574.

Zloty, J. 1996. "A revision of the nearctic *Ameletus* mayflies based on adult males, with descriptions of seven new species (Ephemeroptera: Ameletidae)." *The Canadian Entomologist* 128:293–346.

Zuellig, R. E., B. C. Kondratieff, and H. A. Rhodes. 2002. "Benthos recovery after an episodic sediment release into a Colorado Rocky Mountain river." *Western North American Naturalist:* 62: 59–72.

SUBJECT INDEX

Page numbers in italics indicate illustrations or tables.

TAXONOMIC INDEX

Page numbers in italics indicate illustrations or tables.